Norse in Newfoundland

A critical examination of archaeological research at the Norse site at L'Anse aux Meadows, Newfoundland

Janet E. Kay

BAR International Series 2339
2012

Published in 2016 by
BAR Publishing, Oxford

BAR International Series 2339

Norse in Newfoundland

ISBN 978 1 4073 0922 4

© J E Kay and the Publisher 2012

The author's moral rights under the 1988 UK Copyright,
Designs and Patents Act are hereby expressly asserted.

All rights reserved. No part of this work may be copied, reproduced, stored,
sold, distributed, scanned, saved in any form of digital format or transmitted
in any form digitally, without the written permission of the Publisher.

BAR Publishing is the trading name of British Archaeological Reports (Oxford) Ltd.
British Archaeological Reports was first incorporated in 1974 to publish the BAR
Series, International and British. In 1992 Hadrian Books Ltd became part of the BAR
group. This volume was originally published by Archaeopress in conjunction with
British Archaeological Reports (Oxford) Ltd / Hadrian Books Ltd, the Series principal
publisher, in 2012. This present volume is published by BAR Publishing, 2016.

Printed in England

BAR titles are available from:

           BAR Publishing
           122 Banbury Rd, Oxford, OX2 7BP, UK
EMAIL   info@barpublishing.com
PHONE +44 (0)1865 310431
  FAX   +44 (0)1865 316916
           www.barpublishing.com

Table of Contents

Introduction	1
CHAPTER 1 The Norse in the North Atlantic and the Vinland Settlement	4
The Longhouse and Traditional Norse Farm	4
Typical Norse Farming Patterns in the North Atlantic	5
Norse Farms in Iceland	5
Norse Farms in Greenland	6
The Vinland Sagas	8
The Quest for Vinland	8
Vinland Settlement Pattern	9
CHAPTER 2 Excavations at L'Anse aux Meadows	10
Location of L'Anse aux Meadows	10
Environmental Context	13
Building Construction	15
Complex A-B-C: Archaeological Description	15
Complex A-B-C: Archaeological Analysis	21
Complex D-E: Archaeological Description	22
Complex D-E: Archaeological Analysis	28
Complex F-G: Archaeological Description	29
Complex F-G: Archaeological Analysis	35
The Smithy (Building J): Archaeological Description and Analysis	37
Charcoal Kiln and Cooking Pits: Archaeological Description and Analysis	38
Boat Sheds: Archaeological Description and Analysis	41
Analysis of Building Construction	41
Conclusion of Site Layout and Excavations	42
CHAPTER 3 Artifact Evidence and Analyses	44
Norse Diagnostic Artifacts	44
Artifact Evidence and the Origins of the Inhabitants of L'Anse aux Meadows	44
Artifact Dating	45
Domestic Artifacts	45
Carpentry Debris and Wooden Artifacts	46
Iron Smelting and Smithing	47
Boat Repair	49
Purpose and Central Activity of the Site	50
CHAPTER 4: Dietary and Agricultural Practices at L'Anse aux Meadows	51
Dietary Adaptations to the North Atlantic: Iceland	51
Dietary Adaptations to the North Atlantic: Greenland	52
Dietary Practices at L'Anse aux Meadows	53
Livestock at L'Anse aux Meadows	54
Palynological Studies	55
Hearth Evidence and Cooking Structures	57
Norse Diet at L'Anse aux Meadows	58
CHAPTER 5 Site Occupation and Social Analysis	59
Radiocarbon Dating	59
Architectural Evidence: Occupation Date and Length	60
Population Size	61
Social Structure	61
Women at L'Anse aux Meadows	62
Women and Weaving in the Norse North Atlantic	63
Weaving in Hut E	64
CONCLUSION	66
Acknowledgements	67
Bibliography	68

List of Figures

Fig. 1.1 Diagram of House 1 at Jarlshof — 5

Fig. 1.2, Stöng house-site in Þjórsárdalur, Iceland — 6

Fig. 1.3, House at Narssaq, East Settlement, Greenland — 7

Fig. 1.4a, The dwelling at the North Farm at Brattahlid — 7

Fig. 1.4b, The well in Room VI in the North Farm dwelling at Brattahlid — 8

Fig. 1.4c, The dwelling at the River Farm, Brattahlid — 8

Fig. 2.1a, Location of Newfoundland in North Atlantic — 11

Fig. 2.1b, Location map of L'Anse aux Meadows on the island of Newfoundland — 12

Fig. 2.1c, Location map of Épaves Bay and L'Anse aux Meadows — 12

Fig. 2.2a Plan of the archaeological site at L'Anse aux Meadows by Ingstad — 13

Fig. 2.2b Plan of the site at L'Anse aux Meadows by Wallace — 14

Fig. 2.3, Photo of strengur technique used in L'Anse aux Meadows reconstructions — 15

Fig. 2.4a, Plan of Complex A-B-C by Ingstad — 16

Fig. 2.4b, Plan of Complex A-B-C with artifact placement by Wallace — 17

Fig. 2.5, Photo of excavated Hall A from the east — 17

Fig. 2.6 Photo of post hole in the west end of Room II, Hall A — 17

Fig. 2.7, Photo of cooking pit in Room III, Hall A. Post hole to the right of pit — 18

Fig. 2.8, Ring-headed pin from Hall A, Room III, length 6.7 cm — 18

Fig. 2.9, Photo from the east of the space between Hall A and structures B and C, displaying early summer flood — 19

Fig. 2.10, Photo of excavated House B from the east, showing the hearths — 19

Fig. 2.11, Photo of the large hearth in House B — 19

Fig. 2.12, Plan of House B by Ingstad — 20

Fig. 2.13a, Photo of the cooking pit of House B, with large hearth in back — 20

Fig. 2.13b, Profile of cooking Pit in House B — 20

Fig. 2.14, Photo of the ember pit in House B — 21

Fig. 2.15, Large hearth opposite the door in Room I at the North Farm of Brattahlid — 22

Fig. 2.16a, Plan of Complex D-E by Ingstad   23

Fig. 2.16b, Plan of Complex D-E with artifact distribution by Wallace   24

Fig. 2.17a, Plan of Room III, Hall D   25

Fig. 2.17b, Photo of Room III, Hall D   25

Fig. 2.18, Photo of the long hearth with ember pit in Room III, Hall D   26

Fig 2.19, Glass bead (1.05 cm) from outside the east wall of Hall D, Room III   26

Fig. 2.20, Photo of hearth in Hut E, with post hole to the left   26

Fig. 2.21, Plan of Hut E by Ingstad, Note the two 'post holes' on either side of the hearth   27

Fig. 2.22, Plan of Complex F-G by Wallace   30

Fig. 2.23, Plan of Hall F by Ingstad   31

Fig. 2.24, Photo of Hall F from the northeast   31

Fig. 2.25a, Long hearth with cooking pit, ember pit, and flat stone in Room II, Hall F   32

Fig. 2.25b Plan and section of hearth in Room II, Hall F   32

Fig. 2.26, Photo of ember pit of the long hearth in Room II, Hall F   33

Fig. 2.27, Photo of Room VI, Hall F, from the southwest, showing wooden impressions in floor   34

Fig. 2.28, Needle hone from Hall F, Room VI, 7.3 cm long by 0.7 cm section   34

Fig. 2.29, Plan and section of House G by Ingstad   36

Fig. 2.30a, Photo of Smithy seen from the river, with the charcoal kiln in the back left   37

Fig. 2.30b, Photo of Smithy prior to Parks Canada excavations, 1975   37

Fig. 2.31a, Plan of Smithy by Eldjárn   38

Fig. 2.32, Stone anvil in Smithy   38

Fig. 2.31b, Wallace's plan of Smithy J   39

Fig. 2.33a, Plan of Cooking Pit I   40

Fig. 2.33b, Photo of Cooking Pit I   40

Fig. 2.34a, Photo of Cooking Pit II   40

Fig. 2.34b, Plan of Cooking Pit II   40

Fig. 2.35, Photo of the reconstruction of Complex A-B-C at the National Parks Site at L'Anse aux Meadows   43

Fig. 3.1, The only whole nail found on the site 44

Fig. 3.2, Copper fragment from Hall D, Room III 44

Fig. 3.3 Bone needle from Hall D 44

Fig. 3.4, Jasper strike-a-lights from L'Anse aux Meadows 45

Fig. 3.5, The spindle whorl from L'Anse aux Meadows 46

Fig. 3.6 Several examples of spindle whorls found at Jarlshof 46

Fig. 3.7, Weights from Jarlshof, (1–8, soapstone loom weights, 9–10 soapstone fishing weights) 46

Fig. 3.8, Sandstone fishing weights from Jarlshof 46

Fig. 3.9, Small birchbark container found in the bog 47

Fig. 3.10, Coiled spruce roots 47

Fig. 5.1, Faroese warp-weighted loom 63

Fig. 5.2, Bone needles from Jarlshof 64

Fig. 5.3, Spindle whorls of soapstone and spindles of wood from farms in the Western Settlement of Greenland 64

Fig. 5.4a, Spinning and twining hook of wood, found in the Farm Beneath the Sand 64

Fig. 5.4b, Loom weights from the Farm Beneath the Sand 64

INTRODUCTION

Explorer Helge Ingstad set out in the 1960s to search for the much hypothesized and mythical Norse land of Vinland. Vinland, originally discovered by Leif Erikson c. 1000 CE, is described in two sagas written in the thirteenth century: the *Saga of the Greenlanders* and the *Saga of Erik the Red*. These sagas mention a land that appeared to be congruent with a description of northern Newfoundland. In his search, Helge Ingstad and his wife, Anne Stine Ingstad, came across a site in L'Anse aux Meadows, Newfoundland, which seemed to fit the description of Vinland.

Anne Stine Ingstad led archaeological expeditions to L'Anse aux Meadows over seven seasons from 1961–1968, conducting excavations which uncovered buildings and features "of a type which makes it clear to anyone familiar with Norse archaeology that this must have been a Norse settlement" (A.S. Ingstad 1985a, 28). Excavations resumed in the 1970s for the National Historic Parks and Sites Branch, Parks Canada, under the direction of Birgitta Wallace, who had been a member of the Ingstad archaeological team. The project focused on the re-excavation of the sod structures and on the investigation of their surroundings, in an effort to prepare the ruins for restoration and preservation as an interpretive archaeological site within a national park. The three excavation seasons—1973–1976, 2000, and 2002—concentrated particularly on the terrace and peat bog. Wallace concluded that the site was undoubtedly Norse and dated to the end of the tenth century CE.

A substantial amount of information can be determined from the archaeological remains at L'Anse aux Meadows; preservation conditions on the sandy terrace, however, leave much to be desired. Thus, the question arises of how to interpret the remains in light of the meager artifact evidence. The possibility of text-aided archaeology remains, for the sagas that led Helge Ingstad to discover the site in 1961 could provide a source of comparison for questions that purely archaeological data cannot answer. The problem with traditional methods of interpretation of the archaeological site at L'Anse aux Meadows stems from two main issues: the atypical nature of the site and the poor preservation conditions on the terrace above Épaves Bay. The latter increases the possibility of the destruction of artifact evidence which could illuminate activities at the site. The site's atypical nature presents larger issues, especially when combined with the meager artifact evidence in contrast with contemporary Norse sites. Much of the knowledge about Norse life comes from excavations of Norse farms. L'Anse aux Meadows, however, is not an agricultural settlement based on farming. It is therefore difficult to determine the extent to which the archaeological remains can be compared to contemporary sites elsewhere in the North Atlantic and Scandinavia.

An alternative method to comparison with contemporary sites is the use of the Vinland Sagas as guides to explaining life at L'Anse aux Meadows—after all, it was Helge Ingstad's study of the sagas which led to the discovery of the site. At L'Anse aux Meadows, however, the texts which could serve as background information deal with activities from a millennium ago, and there is no way to confirm their factual accuracy. Wallace emphasizes that *literal* translations of the sagas are "futile," as they are not "straightforward accounts of actual events," even though they may contain some historical facts (Wallace 1990, 166). The Vinland Sagas have been debated by experts in Norse epic literature and languages for the last two hundred years (the debate over the word and its vowels and meaning will not be discussed in this paper); the conclusion of much of this scholarship is that some general themes may be reliable, but they cannot be trusted to the extent that historical archaeology has traditionally relied on texts.

The sagas, however, must be taken into account when interpreting the archaeological record at L'Anse aux Meadows. The Ingstads focused their analysis on proving that the site was, in fact, a Norse site dating to the end of the first millennium. The majority of excavated Norse sites, however, are agricultural settlements, which is not the case at L'Anse aux Meadows. For analysis of the site, one must therefore find another pattern of settlement with which to compare the ruins on Épaves Bay. In this context, considering broader outlines and general themes, Wallace suggested using the sagas anthropologically, for "regardless of their historicity, the descriptions contain interrelated variables that depict the structural system of the Vinland expeditions as well as the correlated subsystems" (Wallace 1990, 166–7). Wallace created a model of settlement pattern for the storied Vinland expeditions, to which she compared the Norse site at L'Anse aux Meadows. As the Vinland sagas describe voyages across the North Atlantic to Canada, and Ingstad had determined that L'Anse aux Meadows is a Norse site, the broader themes of the sagas can be taken into account when definitive answers cannot be deduced from the archaeological record.

A number of controversial issues surround the site in addition to the accuracy of the sagas. The majority of Ingstad's research dealt with proving that the buildings at L'Anse aux Meadows were indeed of Norse origin. The site is undoubtedly Norse, in hindsight; at the time of excavation, however, archaeological investigation seemed to focus on finding evidence of Norse occupation rather than collecting all evidence available at the site. Macrobotanical samples, which could have provided a wealth of information about the people at the site's dietary practices, were not collected. Additionally, the published data is not complete, and it is difficult to tell where the gaps in the record result from oversights in excavation and when they simply reflect incomplete publication. The Parks Canada excavations were careful to continue and expand upon Ingstad's investigations, but the reports of these later excavations have not been published, and all information available comes from Wallace's articles. Thus, the resulting dependence on secondary documents limits interpretation of the site.

In this study, the published archaeological reports from the Ingstad and Wallace excavations are critically examined, in conjunction with supplementary background and comparative studies, to determine how the settlement at L'Anse aux Meadows functioned, and what its general purpose was. In particular its focus is dietary practices and site activities. Available archaeological evidence indicates that the site at L'Anse aux Meadows was a temporary base camp for further exploration into North America, and that traditional Norse agricultural methods were not implemented at the site. The sole activity for which there is conclusive evidence in the archaeological remains is boat repair, seen in the recovery of iron slag, the excavation of the boat sheds, and the evidence for the forging and use of iron nails at the site.

Prior to this study, the conclusions that Ingstad and Wallace drew about the presence of women at L'Anse aux Meadows were based on interpretation of several small artifacts in light of the Vinland Sagas, which mention the presence of women. In an archaeological context previously undiscussed, however, indicates that at least one woman was present at the site: the presence of stones which could have been used as loom weights in conjunction with post-like indentations in the floor of Hut E. These two small features in the floor, which most likely came from the weight of a large loom leaning against the wall of the hut, indicate that weaving was done in this structure. As weaving was a specifically female activity in the Norse culture, the presence of weaving at this site proves that at least one woman was present at L'Anse aux Meadows.

Chapter 1 provides the reader with background knowledge of typical Norse settlement patterns in the North Atlantic, particularly that of the Norse farm; specific examples of Norse farms in the Shetlands, Iceland, and Greenland will be discussed. The Vinland Sagas, and the extent to which they can be used when interpreting archaeological evidence, are also discussed.

Chapter 2 concerns the location and layout of the Norse site at L'Anse aux Meadows. It also provides information on the current environmental conditions at the site. Primarily, Chapter 2 describes the setting, construction, and internal layout of all major structures and features from the Norse occupation. Descriptions of every room and building are consolidated from both the Ingstad and the Parks Canada excavation reports, and particularly focus on the arrangement of hearths and fire features, the construction methods used, and the placement of artifacts within and around each room and structure. The structures and features at L'Anse aux Meadows are compared with contemporary parallels in Greenland, Iceland, and Scandinavia to answer three main questions: who built and lived at the site, for what purpose and activities was it built, and when was it built and for how long did it last.

Chapter 3 deals with artifact evidence and analyses, taking the few artifacts found during excavations and analyzing their probable use. Some, such as the relatively abundant iron nails and carpentry debris, when combined with the building analyses from Chapter 2, indicate that boat repair was one of the main tasks at the site. Certain artifacts indicate that domestic activities were done by the inhabitants of L'Anse aux Meadows, and that at least one woman was present at the site.

Chapter 4 examines the small amount of dietary evidence present at the site to determine which sources of food the Norse obtained and what they may have eaten during their stay at L'Anse aux Meadows. Palynological analyses demonstrate that during the time of Norse occupation, there was no disturbance in the pollen record, and that no attempt was made at large-scale agriculture. Because of a lack of conclusive faunal and macrobotanical evidence, the continuity of climate as evidenced in the palynological record is relied upon to conclude that the Norse most likely had access to the same sources of food as peoples living near L'Anse aux Meadows have today. In this case the Vinland settlement model may be consulted, in order to determine the likelihood of the presence of livestock on the site during the Norse occupation, in conjunction with the possible evidence for their presence based upon building layouts.

Introduction

The radiocarbon evidence discussed in Chapter 5 indicates that the Norse occupied the site at the turn of the first millennium, the time period in which Leif Erikson is said to have sailed to Vinland. The aggregation of evidence presented in favor of Wallace's Vinland settlement model thus allows its use to determine exactly who lived at L'Anse aux Meadows and how the social structure operated. In particular, the artifact evidence will be analyzed in light of Norse tradition to conclusively prove that there was a female presence at the site, which also coincides with the Vinland settlement model.

CHAPTER 1 The Norse in the North Atlantic and the Vinland Settlement

The chapter presents the reader with background knowledge of the traditional Norse longhouse and farm, as well as a brief summation of the Vinland Sagas and Wallace's Vinland settlement model.

The Longhouse and Traditional Norse Farm

In order to understand the similarities in construction and use of the buildings at L'Anse aux Meadows with those at contemporary Norse sites, the traditional building models must be understood; during the Viking period, "the same type of house was transported abroad to the new settlements," including those in Iceland and Greenland (Shetelig and Falk 1978, 320). Thus, buildings in Iceland and Greenland may serve as models for comparison for the Norse settlement at L'Anse aux Meadows, and the following analyses focus on these two Norse colonies. Indeed, the identification of L'Anse aux Meadows as a Norse site is based largely on information derived from building construction, combined with the scant but compelling artifact evidence.

The Icelandic word *skálar* (pl. *skáli*) refers to a particular type of large, long, and rectangular hall. This type of house dates to the beginning of Icelandic settlement around 900 CE, but derives from an earlier Scandinavian form, "with the specific Icelandic modification that no room was made for large domestic animals" (Gad 1970, 36). One of a number of buildings on a typical early farm, the *skálar* was used as a dwelling for people—animals had their own separate, smaller outbuildings for shelter (A.S. Ingstad 1985c, 169). A single entrance from the outside, usually on the end of the *skálar*, would serve the entire house and all of its rooms. Inside the typical entrance was a small storage room or closet. At the end of the house opposite the entrance would have been the small bedrooms used by the owner of the house and his guests (Jóhannesson 2006, 339).

The *skálar* could be divided by wooden partitions and if additional space was necessary, new rooms would be constructed at the ends of the house, forming a large complex of rooms in a single row (A.S. Ingstad 1985c, 164). The large hall in the center of the *skálar* would have had raised benches along the walls, with a long hearth in the center to provide light and heat to the hall (Jóhannesson 2006, 339). The position and form of the hearth(s) in the *skálar* are important criteria to the identification of this type of building (A.S. Ingstad 1985c, 195). Simple hearths of this type are also "quite common" at early settlements in Greenland (A.S. Ingstad 1985, 165), where cooking pits "are among the most common types of hearths" (A.S. Ingstad 1985, 167–9). Though the long hearth is one of the main factors for identification, other cooking pits would have been constructed throughout the hall. The largest cooking-pit would face the entrance and was typically protected from the draught by means of upright stones (Gad 1970, 38). Between the benches and the hearth, supporting the roof, would stand a double row of wooden posts, one on either side of the hearth. People sat, ate, and slept on these benches, and certain areas of the bench would be designated for groups of different social status (Jóhannesson 2006, 339).

Roofs were supported by rows of posts running parallel to the long hearths and the longest walls; smaller houses tended to have one row, while larger halls have two. Each row of posts was connected by a wooden beam along the length of the roof line, and when there were two rows, each pair of posts was joined by cross-beams. Above these cross-beams, parallel to the length of the house, ran a ridge-beam, which was placed at the center of the roof. The roof itself would include two layers: the inner, directly on top of the roof beams, made of bark or planks, and the outer one made of turf (Shetelig and Falk 1978, 322).

These longhouses were common on all Norse settlements in the North Atlantic, particularly Iceland and Greenland. The Greenlanders, however, made their own specific adaptations to the basic *skálar* plan based on their surroundings. One main question surrounding the buildings at L'Anse aux Meadows entails the country of origin for each building, to determine from which Scandinavian outpost the settlers arrived. Therefore, knowledge of the specific adaptations in Greenland is crucial.

The problem Greenlanders specifically dealt with in the traditional *skálar* house-type was the proper heating of the house, as a result of the increased difficulty in obtaining fuel compared to Iceland (Ingstad and Ingstad 2000, 15); therefore, the *skáli* in Greenland changed early in the settlement period (Gad 1970, 38). Greenland houses were constructed from the same materials as Icelandic houses—turf and stone—but they soon evolved into two distinct structural styles, both of which differ dramatically from the traditional *skálar* longhouse. *Passage houses* were built when small rooms were added along either side of a long corridor, and *centralized houses* were a maze-like complex of rooms, in which all rooms led into other rooms within one large structure. The major difference between the two, however, was that *passage* houses were solely for human occupation and were surrounding by outbuildings used for other purposes, while *centralized* houses incorporated the outbuildings into one large structure along with the main dwelling. Although several examples of traditional *skáli* were constructed during the initial settlement of Greenland—Hvalsey, the Farm Beneath the Sand, Narssaq, and Brattahlið—most of the later houses were of the passage and centralized types (Ingstad and Ingstad 2000, 15).

Early Icelandic sites are characterized by the presence of two or more longhouses, all apparently contemporary. Typically, the longhouse, as the main dwelling of a settlement, was flanked by smaller outbuildings that served the specific functions of the farm. Initial settlement began with the construction of a pithouse, to be used as a temporary shelter during the construction of larger buildings; after the permanent longhouse was constructed, these temporary buildings were left to serve another purpose or to collapse. If these pithouses had any features at all, they commonly had a fireplace (Vésteinsson 2000, 168). The longhouse usually contained the main room and other small adjoining rooms; if an Icelandic farm complex had a "sitting room," it could usually be found within or attached to the longhouse and not as a separate building; these sitting rooms were typically used for social gatherings rather than cooking or storage (Jóhannesson 2006, 341). In Greenland, in contrast, the development of a *centralized house* entailed the aggregation of living rooms, storage rooms, a smithy, and livestock byres into one large house (Ingstad and Ingstad 2000, 15).

Typical Norse Farming Patterns in the North Atlantic
Norse farms typically consisted of the *skálar* and smaller buildings used for particular functions; occasionally, these smaller structures were connected to the main house, and they could be set on ground level or dug into the earth. Byres for livestock were normally set far away from the *skálar*, though they were sometimes connected in mountainous regions (Rafnsson 1997, 124). The Greenland *centralized house* presents an odd exception to this rule; in general, the Norse farm complex consisted of several smaller buildings surrounding family gardens and the longhouse (Wallace 2000c, 211).

The Norse arrived at Jarlshof, on the southern tip of Shetland, in the early 9th century CE and lived there through the 14th century CE. For the purposes of this paper, the initial phases of settlement (ending in the 10th century CE) are of particular importance, in order to supply comparative data for the foundation of a site at L'Anse aux Meadows. In the earliest phases of construction they constructed three longhouses (Houses 1, 2, and 3) in a manner of construction similar to the *skáli* of early Icelandic settlement (Fig. 1.1); they measured roughly 21 m in length and were of a construction layout later termed the "*Þjórsárdalur-type*," to be discussed below (Hamilton 1956, 102). Several small outbuildings were also constructed during this phase of site occupation, some of which were identified as a smithy, bathhouse, barn, and byre. All of the buildings at Jarlshof were constructed from turf and stone, dwellings and outbuildings alike, and the longhouses had roofs supported by two rows of post holes (Hamilton 1956, 102–3). Thus, it appears that at the end of the first millennium, the Norse settlement at Jarlshof had established itself as a farm whose inhabitants relied upon animal husbandry and agriculture for their diet and gave fishing "a relatively minor role" (Hamilton 1956, 94). They lived in three large Icelandic-type *skáli* and had several outbuildings for keeping livestock and working iron.

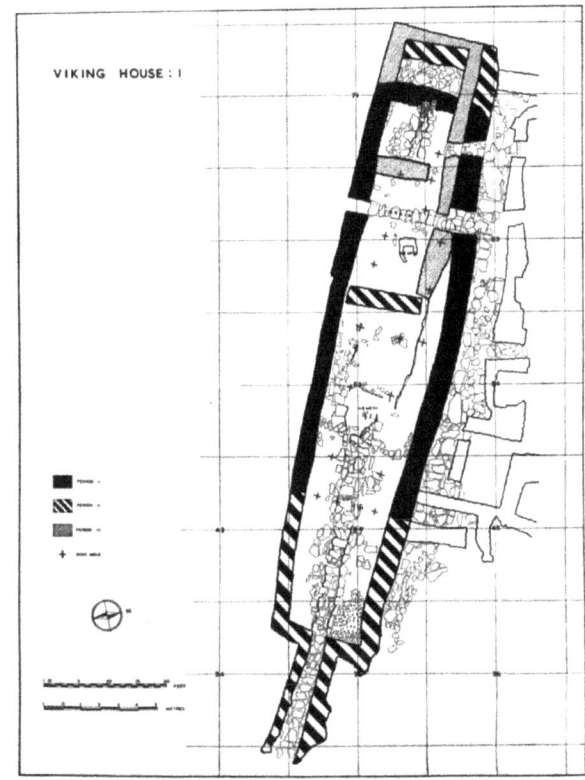

1.1 Diagram of House 1 at Jarlshof (After Hamilton 1956, 108)

Norse Farms in Iceland
Icelandic homesteads had a stable (*stallr*) and a byre (*féhus, fjós*) for the sheep, goats, and cattle (Shetelig and Falk 1978, 325). The byre was divided into separate stalls by rows of wooden posts, and the resulting corridor in the center of the building was used for drainage of manure and urine (Shetelig and Falk 1978, 325–6). The Icelandic

climate allowed sheep and horses to remain in open pasture for most of the year, though the *fjárborg*, a round hut with a domed-roof, gave protection from bad weather (Shetelig and Falk 1978, 326); the animals grazed in the meadows, and were only occasionally fed with surplus hay. In bad years, the lack of supplies sometimes necessitated that these animals be slaughtered (Buckland 2000, 147). Such practice remains common in modern Iceland, where "the sheep are so hardy that in some sections of the country they can be left outdoors the year around, although of course they must be rounded up twice a year—once for shearing and once for slaughtering" (Rothery 1948, 43). Cattle were sent out to graze in the fields during the winter, and were driven into the mountain pastures in the summer (Jóhannesson 2006, 290). As the tenth century passed in Iceland, and the initial forests disappeared through the *landnám* settlement process into meadows—which provided more fodder for their livestock—the pigs and goats so commonly left to forage in the forests were slowly replaced by cows.

Barns, for the storing of agricultural equipment as well as hay and unthreshed grain, were not typically necessary in Iceland; early in the settlement, it was determined that Iceland provided less suitable conditions for the growing of grain than did the Scandinavian homelands. Thus animal husbandry became proportionally more important to Icelandic agriculture (Jóhannesson 2006, 288). Each homestead generally had a barn (*hlaða*); the roof of the barn could be adjusted on a pole, to make more storage room. Similar to the byre, the barn was divided into side-spaces (*golf*) and the central threshing-floor (*láfi*), with its floor of boards or hard clay, by a double row of posts. These outbuildings usually lay separate from the dwellings, arranged in an orderly manner (Shetelig and Falk 1978, 326).

A specifically early Icelandic type of building layout comes from sites such as the Stöng farm in the Þjórsárdalur valley (Fig. 1.2) (Buckland 2008, 600). The "*Þjórsárdalur-type*" of longhouse consisted of a lobby, a sleeping hall, and a *stofa*, or living room, all built in a row, with one or two rooms added onto the long side-walls of the house (A.S. Ingstad 1985c, 198). Ingstad noted there are no direct parallels between the Þjórsárdalur house and any house in Greenland (A.S. Ingstad 1985c, 198–9).

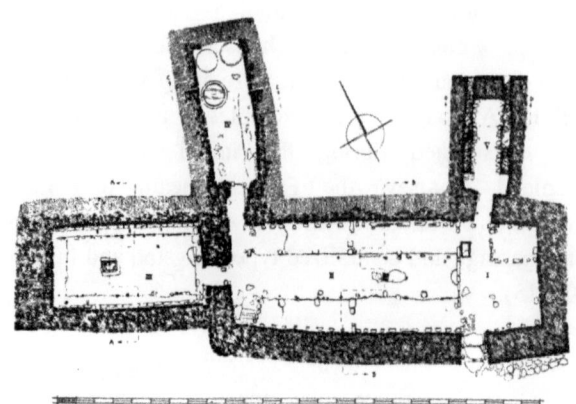

Fig. 1.2, Stöng house-site in Þjórsárdalur, Iceland. (After A. Roussell. in A. Ingstad 1985c, 198)

Norse Farms in Greenland

Closer to Newfoundland, Greenland was a colonizing venture based on agriculture. The people who moved from Iceland to this large, inhospitable landmass in the North Atlantic "attempted to maintain the lifestyle they had known in Iceland, keeping herds of sheep and cows and even horses" (Ólafsson 2000, 145). As in Iceland, the supply of fodder such as seaweed, grass, and leaf hay gathered during the summer dictated the number of animals that could be kept alive over the winter (Buckland 2000, 147). In order to survive in the harsher climate, however, the Norse could live in Greenland "only by exploiting every possible means of subsistence" (Ingstad and Ingstad 2000, 9). Home fields were irrigated and manured, and seaweed, moss, and grass growing amongst rocks were gathered for fodder and food (Ingstad and Ingstad 2000, 16).

The farm at Narssaq in the East Settlement consists of one *skáli* and nine other outbuildings constructed in the stone and turf *strengur* method (Fig. 1.3) (Albrethson 2000, 98). The large hall represents the oldest phase, c. 1000 CE (Albrethson 2000, 98). Narssaq's construction followed practices observed in the North since the Iron Age: when the house lacked enough space, additional rooms were added to the existing structure, extending its length (A.S. Ingstad 1985c, 164). The entire structure measures 36 m long by 6.5–9 m wide (A.S. Ingstad 1985c, 164), and the hall itself measures 11 m long by 5.5 m wide. The hall contains a long stone hearth down its center, in addition to paved floors and "a system of partially flagged drainage gutters, probably meant to channel rain and meltwater away from the house" (Albrethson 2000, 98). Within this drain was a small barrel which most likely served as a makeshift well (Albrethson 2000, 99)

Fig. 1.3, House at Narssaq, East Settlement, Greenland. (After C.L. Vebaek. in A. Ingstad 1985c, 164)

A similar set of ruins exists as Hvalsey, which was partially excavated in 1935. The site includes a church and a passage house, which centered on Room IX, a hall measuring 14 m by 3.5–4 m and dating to the earliest phase of construction. It contained a central long hearth, a cooking pit in its southeastern corner, and roughly a dozen post holes on either side of the central hearth. There was also a drainage system in the western part of Room IX (Albrethson 2000, 101).

The Farm Beneath the Sand ('Gården under Sandet') in Greenland's Western Settlement was excavated in the 1990s, and had excellent preservation conditions. Of the eight phases of construction at the site, the earliest, for the purposes of this study, is of most interest (c. 1020–1200). This was a hall built of turf walls, measuring 12 m by 5 m internally. The middle of the floor was much lower than its sides, and contained a central long hearth (Albrethson 2000, 104–7). This hearth, 1.7 m long by 0.5 m wide, was "partly edged by vertical flagstones" and was adjacent to an "ashpan"; both were covered by large flat slabs of rocks, which were burnt from use (Albrethson 2000, 105). Two rows of posts on either side of the central hearth supported the roof. The cultural layer above the floor contained few artifacts but many fragments of animal bones, both burnt and unburnt (Albrethson 2000, 105). The cooking pit, 0.5 cm deep and 1 m in diameter, contained peat ash, a piece of a spindle whorl, and a loom weight (Albrethson 107)

Brattahlið, the earliest Norse site in Greenland, is a large farmstead in the Eastern Settlement. It is traditionally understood to have been settled by Erik the Red, and was relied upon heavily by the Ingstads in their analysis of the site at L'Anse aux Meadows. In addition to a church and churchyard, Brattahlið includes two farms dating to the early stages of occupation, the North Farm and the River Farm. Buildings were constructed of turf and stone. The large dwelling of the North Farm (Fig. 1.4a) measures 19.5 m long and 8.7–10 m wide and is divided into six rooms : Room I is a longhall of traditional Norse type, while Rooms II though VI attached to it form a larger passage house, extended as needed over time. The building contains many fireplaces, in addition to a well (Fig. 1.4b) in Room VI at the southern end of the building (Nörlund and Stenberger 1934, 50). Artifacts excavated at the North Farm included spindle whorls and tree-nails, and the faunal assemblage was "remarkably rich in bones of domestic animals as well as seals, whales, and walruses" (Nörlund and Stenberger 1934, 70). The main building at the River Farm, in contrast to the North Farm, is more like the Greenland centralized house in construction, measuring 22 m in width with seven rooms positioned on either side of the long hall (Room I) (Fig. 1.4c). Both farms have stables for cattle, byres, and warehouses (Nörlund and Stenberger 1934).

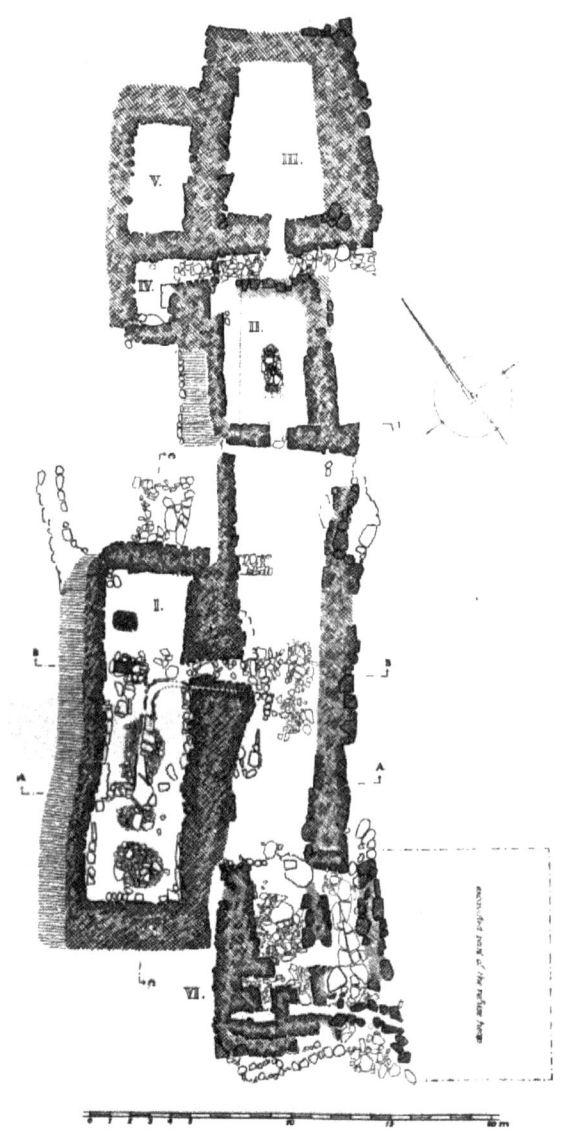

Fig. 1.4a, The dwelling at the North Farm at Brattahlið (After Nörlund and Stenberger 1934, 50)

Fig. 1.4b, The well in Room VI in the North Farm dwelling at Brattahlið (After Nörlund and Stenberger 1934, 55)

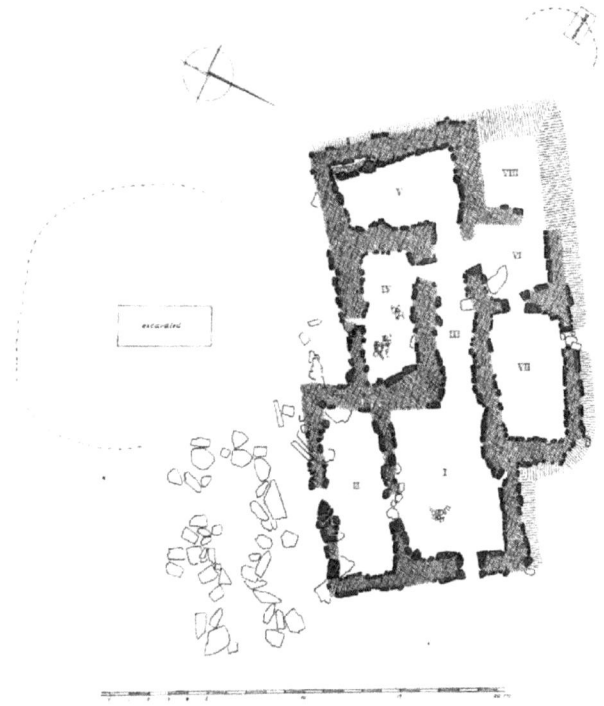

Fig. 1.4c, The dwelling at the River Farm, Brattahlið (After Nörlund and Stenberger 1934, 73)

The Vinland Sagas
The Vinland Sagas include both the *Greenlander's Saga* and the *Saga of Erik the Red*, which were written down in Iceland in the thirteenth century, based upon oral histories of journeys taken to the new world at the turn of the first millennium. They discuss in detail a trip taken to the new land of Vinland, considered to be the perfect farming paradise, where grapes and wheat grew abundantly, where there were plenty of trees and wide forests to produce timber, and where there was much wild game, including fish. Several different ships are described, each led by skipper: Leif Erikson was one, Thorfinn Karlsefni another; the leaders and crews are described as having come from both Iceland and Greenland. Once established in their *buðir* (booths), they began to explore further west, and eventually ran into native peoples, with whom they fought. At the camps, the women took care of daily tasks, cared for the livestock that had been brought, and occasionally defended the camps against native power. Ultimately, the Vinland settlers were forced back to Greenland and Iceland because of their battles with the native inhabitants of Vinland.

Vinland had "plenty of supplies from natural bounty…including grapes, all sorts of game and fish, and other good things" ("The Saga of the Greenlanders" 2008, 15). The sagas mention one site near "fields of self-sown wheat in the low-lying areas and vines growing on the hills" ("Eirik the Red's Saga" 2008, 44), and a second site near the mouth of a bay "where there were strong currents" ("Eirik the Red's Saga" 2008, 42); Large amounts of fish could be found in the rivers, so much that "they dug trenches along the high-water mark and when the tide ebbed there were flounder in them" ("Eirik the Red's Saga" 2008, 44). According to the sagas, the Norse explorers had brought their livestock, and the weather in their new home was good enough that "livestock would need no fodder during the winter. The temperature never dropped below freezing, and the grass only withered very slightly" ("The Saga of the Greenlanders" 2008, 7). In this wonderful land of plenty, they "carried their sleeping-sacks ashore from the ship and built booths. Later they decided to spend the winter there and built large houses" ("The Saga of the Greenlanders" 2008, 7). The search for Vinland, therefore, began with the search for locations which fit the descriptions given in the sagas.

The Quest for Vinland
Early scholarly opinions on the sagas took them at their literal word, and sparked a search for the actual site where Leif Eriksson had landed in North America. The sagas, however, contain not factual information, but rather storied information which reflected the social reality of the day (Lewis-Simpson 2000, 21). As they were first told in the 11th century, but written down independently in Iceland during the 13th century, when literary texts and laws began to be written, "we can never be sure to what extent the picture they give reflects their own time, rather than that of the Viking Age" (Sawyer 2000, "Scandinavia," 51). Sir Magnus Magnusson emphasized that the confusion about certain events in the sagas arises because details "have become blurred and confused with the passage of time and the telling and retelling of the yarns" (Magnusson 2000, 90).

When L'Anse aux Meadows—a site "far too substantial and complex…not to be mentioned in the sagas"—was discovered within the proposed range of Vinland (Wallace 2000b, 380), enthusiasts jumped at the chance to proclaim this part of the North American coast *Vinland*. The question should not be asked, however, whether or not L'Anse aux Meadows *was* Vinland, but whether it was *part* of a larger Vinland. The answer, according to Wallace, is "a resounding 'yes'" (Wallace 2006, 97).

L'Anse aux Meadows is not a typical Norse farming settlement, and comparisons of its structures, features, and artifacts can only be taken to a certain point. Thus, finding a settlement pattern with which it can be compared is essential. Using the sagas as an anthropological source rather than one of historical fact, Wallace created a Vinland settlement pattern based on the general themes and ideas present in the sagas. The acceptance that L'Anse aux Meadows falls within the jurisdiction of the larger area denoted as Vinland thus leads to the conclusion that the site may be compared to the model of settlement suggested by the Vinland sagas, in order to aid interpretation of daily activities at L'Anse aux Meadows when the archaeological record is inconclusive.

- **Vinland Settlement Pattern**

The Vinland manner of settlement was exploratory, using temporary encampments while searching for and exploiting new resources and exploring the potential for permanent settlement at a new site (Wallace 1990, 167). The sagas indicate the Vinland settlement comprised a temporary base camp, *Leifsbúdir*, and two possible outposts, *Straumfjord* and *Hóp* (Wallace 1990, 168). They also state that these temporary expedition camps lasted one full year at least, and a few years at the most (Wallace 1990, 169). In *The Saga of Eric the Red*, several mentions are made of livestock, but not of large amounts. Wallace concluded that though livestock would have been necessary for colonial success, the livestock included on the voyages "must have been brought primarily as part of the overall provisions to provide the dairy products so necessary for a Norse diet" (Wallace 1990, 168).

Explorers would have most likely sailed in the large merchant vessels known as *knarrir*, the size of which determined the number of people who could be taken on such a voyage; the use of these *knarrir* as transport thus indicates that the people who sailed them were wealthy, as their construction and operation required "a substantial financial investment" (Wallace 1990, 167). Each ship, based upon its size, could have held 20 to 35 individuals, not including cargo; this then gives an estimate on how many people would have been present at a Vinland site, given in multiples, depending on how many ships sailed together as part of an expedition.

Though the individual people who sailed to Vinland cannot be historically documented, Wallace (Wallace 1990, 167) interprets the sagas to infer a social hierarchy among the members of the crew:

(1) The skipper, with or without his or her spouse
(2) Partners of the skipper
(3) Personal retainers or domestics of the skipper
(4) Freemen working for a share in the profit;
(5) Female domestics
(6) Slaves

The freemen constituted the majority of the crew, and though "male crew members usually provided their own food and did their own cooking on voyages," the unknown potential for settlement in Vinland allowed for the inclusion of women in the Vinland voyages; Wallace considered it "logical that a few females would have been included to handle the food preparation, general housekeeping, and clothing maintenance" (Wallace 1990, 167). The expeditions were therefore led by the wealthy owner of the ship which brought them to Vinland, and which was attended by a crew mainly comprising men, with the occasional woman.

This background knowledge is essential for the interpretation and further discussion of the archaeological ruins discovered at L'Anse aux Meadows. The *skáli* are common structures on Norse sites in the North Atlantic, especially in Iceland and Greenland; these main dwellings were typically surrounded by smaller outbuildings. Each Norse area of settlement had its own particular variations in building construction and agricultural methods to ensure survival in the North Atlantic. The Vinland settlement pattern, as created by Wallace, in contrast, displays none of the typical Norse methods of permanent settlement. Shelters were temporary, agriculture was virtually nonexistent, and wild game and other resources supplied the diet. The Norse pattern of farm settlement, in contrast to the Vinland model, must be kept in mind for the analysis of building use in the following chapter.

CHAPTER 2 Excavations at L'Anse aux Meadows

The location of the Norse site at L'Anse aux Meadows within the greater North Atlantic region, as well as its local topography, must be understood before archaeological interpretation occurs, as climate and environmental conditions limit the type of work that could be conducted at the site and set the framework for analysis. This chapter summarizes the results of archaeological investigations of the three structural complexes at L'Anse aux Meadows, as well as the larger outdoor features and the boat sheds. It describes and analyzes the layout and construction of each building and room, including hearths, artifacts, and other features and compares them to other Norse sites in the North Atlantic.

Location of L'Anse aux Meadows

The archaeological site of L'Anse aux Meadows lies at the northernmost point of the Great Northern Promontory in Newfoundland, next to a small village of the same name (Fig. 2.1a, 2.1b, and 2.1c). At latitude 51°35' N and longitude 53°32' W (A.S. Ingstad 1985a, 25), cool summer temperatures seldom rise above 77°F (25°C), and in the cold winters, roughly 70 cm of snowfall can be expected, with temperatures dipping to 14.9°F (9.5°C) (Schonback et. al. 1976, 7).

The site is surrounded by extensive meadows, which are characteristic of the larger region. Pollen analysis indicates that neither climate nor vegetation has changed noticeably in the past millennium, and that the environment appears today as it would have to Norse settlers in the eleventh century. L'Anse aux Meadows in fact bears a "striking resemblance to western Norway, Iceland and other areas occupied by West Norse peoples" (Schonback et. al. 1976, 7); settlement areas in Iceland were often positioned on or near wetlands, which saved early settlers from the need to clear forests (Vésteinsson 2000, 171). It was this modern environment that so drew Helge Ingstad in his search for Norse sites along the North Atlantic coast of Canada: "It struck me that it was just at such a place that Norsemen would choose to settle: they had meadows about with food for their cattle and they had an outlook over both sea and land. Much reminded me of the locations of the Norse dwellings in Greenland" (Ingstad 1971, 178).

Anne Stine Ingstad and Birgitta Wallace clearly demonstrated that the Norse had indeed reached the northern coast of Newfoundland. The site at L'Anse aux Meadows lies 70–100 meters inland from Épaves Bay, on a curving beach terrace 4 meters above the water (Fig. 2.2a and 2.2b) (A.S. Ingstad 1985a, 27), on "the only dry ground between a funnel-shaped sedge-peat bog and a tussocky, raised sphagnum-moss bog" (Wallace 2000c, 209). Épaves Bay accumulates "considerable quantities" of driftwood, allowing a ready source of fuel for those living in the vicinity (A.S. Ingstad 1985a, 255). In the eleventh century, prior to land uplift and a dip in sea level, the bay was most likely even more favorable for boats, and the settlement on the terrace would have been closer to the shoreline (Wallace 1990, 170). The terrace consists of sand and gravel, covered by a thin (5–10 cm thick) layer of humus, and is mostly devoid of stone (A.S. Ingstad 1985a, 27); it is divided into two parts by Black Duck Brook, which encircles a peat bog to the south before dividing the terrace and running into the bay (Wallace 1977, "Norse," 4).

The archaeological ruins of seven structures lie to the east of Black Duck Brook; they are situated in small clusters of two or three, which appear to be separate complexes, each comprising one larger hall and one or two smaller one-roomed huts. The complexes lie in a north-south alignment on the terrace, consistently distanced from each other by about thirty meters.

Hall A lies furthest south on the terrace, bounded by Black Duck Brook on its southern and western sides. House B and C lie between the southern wall of Hall A and the brook, with House B east of Hut C. The brook, after flowing west past Hut C, veers sharply north for about 30 meters before turning. On the western corner of this turn lies Building J, interpreted as the Smithy. After the turn, the brook flows east for another 30 meters, before veering north again to join Épaves Bay. North of Complex A-B-C on the same terrace lies Hall D, with Hut E on its northern side. Still to the north is Hut G with large Hall F to its northern side. All three Halls and their Complexes—A-B-C, D-E, and F-G—overlook Épaves Bay to the northwest, and are bounded to the southeast by the bog. Also present on the terrace are several large features that bear mentioning: a charcoal kiln and a hearth outside the Smithy (Building J) on the western bank of Black Duck Brook; four man-made depressions on the shoreline north of the Smithy interpreted as boatsheds; a cooking pit where the brook meets the bay; and a second cooking pit northwest of Hall F.

Excavations at L'Anse aux Meadows

Fig. 2.1a, Location of Newfoundland in North Atlantic (circled) (Google Earth, 2011)

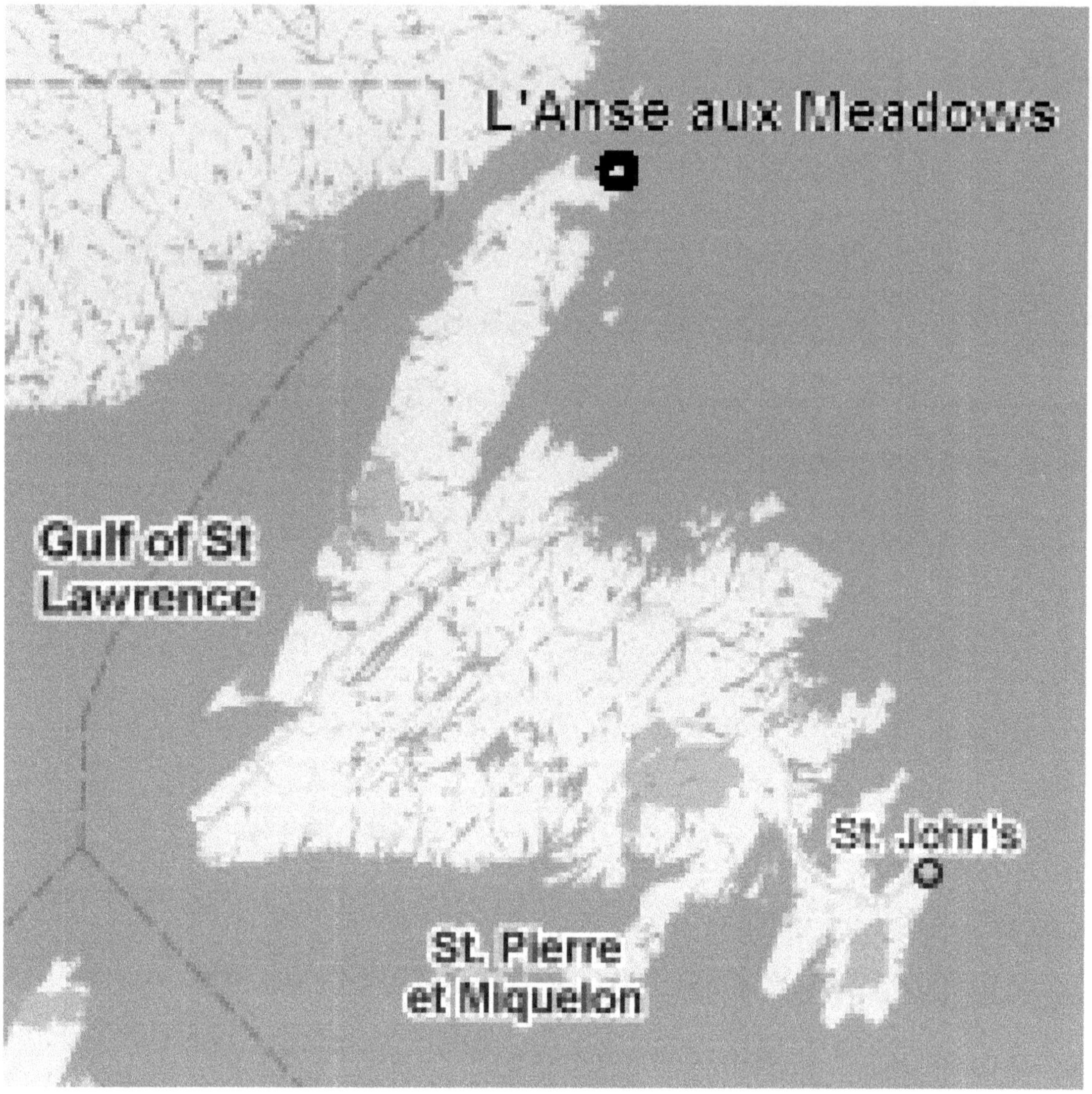

Fig. 2.1b, Location map of L'Anse aux Meadows on the island of Newfoundland (Google Maps 2011)

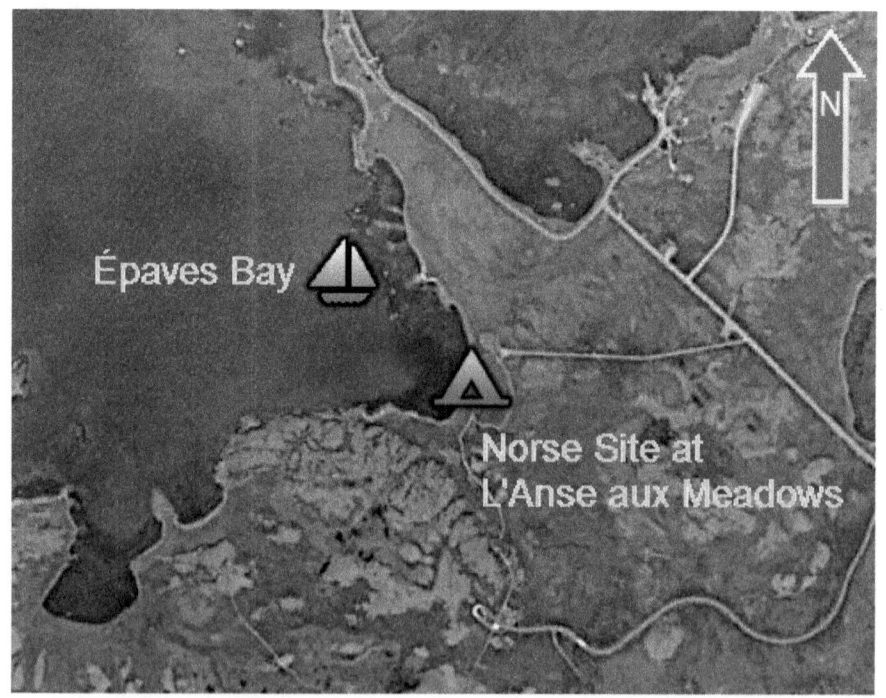

Fig. 2.1c, Location map of Épaves Bay and L'Anse aux Meadows. (Google Earth 2011)

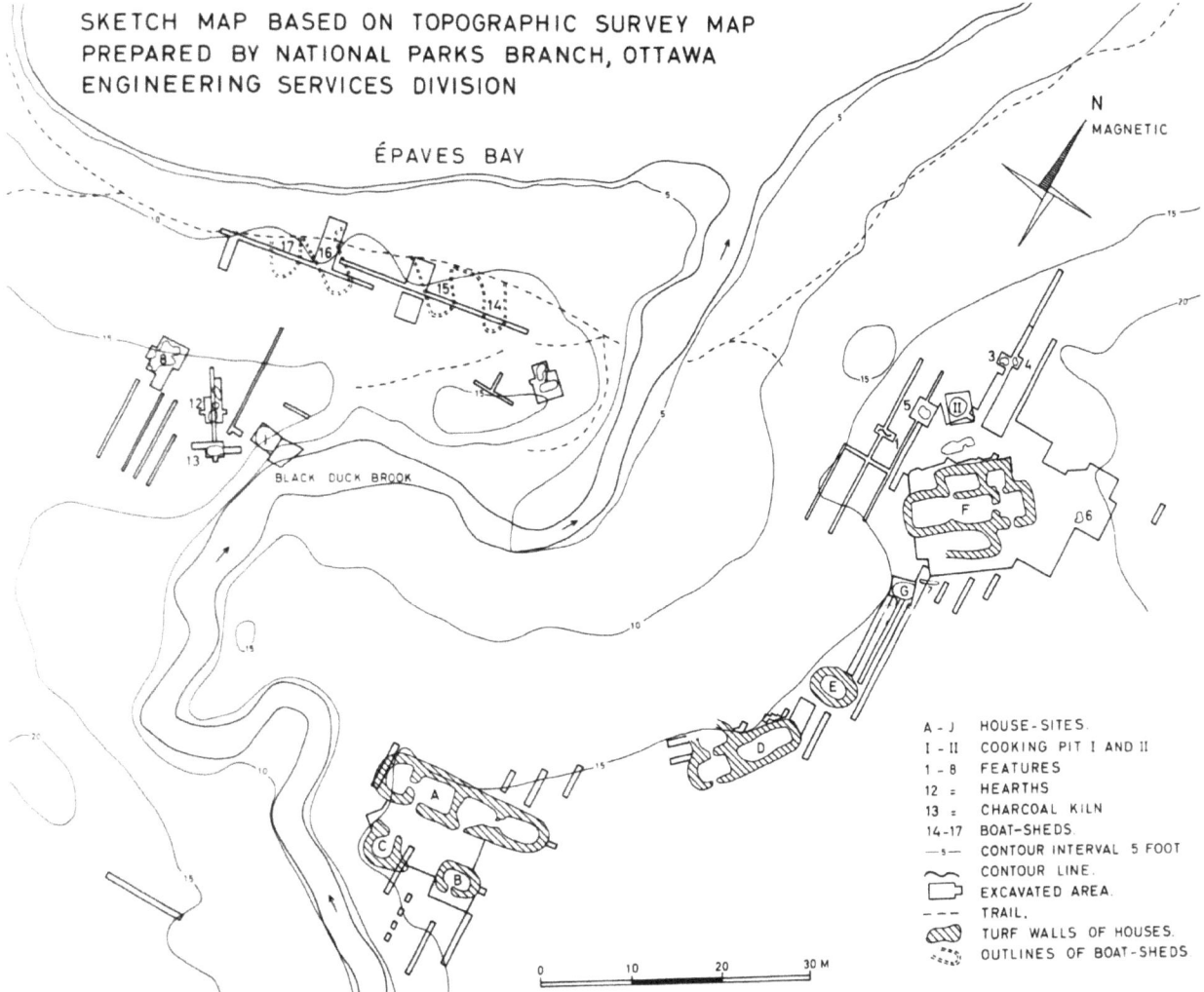

Fig. 2.2a Plan of the archaeological site at L'Anse aux Meadows by Ingstad (After A.S. Ingstad 1985, Pl. 2)

Environmental Context

The terrace itself consists mostly of peat bog, and evidence within the walls of the turf structures indicates that the bog was "considerably wetter during the Norse period" (Wallace 2000a, 171). The perfect preservation of some of the wood fragments found in the peat indicates that the bog once held standing water, most likely from the stripping of the sod peat, which would have made conditions in the bog even wetter (Wallace 2000a, 171).

Though the bog provided decent conditions for the preservation of wood materials, very few other artifacts survived on the site. Organic preservation is poor in the majority of early Norse sites excavated (Vésteinsson 2000, 169), and L'Anse aux Meadows is no exception; all remains of organic material within the turf structures, except for a few slivers of burnt bone and charcoal, have been destroyed by the chemical condition of the sandy terrace. Ingstad emphasized that many of the tools used by the Norse were made of antler, wood, and bone, and would have survived in the peat but not within the buildings. Thus, their absence from the living and working areas of the site is not unexpected. Post holes, however, were well preserved (A.S. Ingstad 1985d, 261).

Additionally, water levels at L'Anse aux Meadows have changed over time. Black Duck Brook, which cuts through the terrace between the Complexes and the Smithy, floods periodically. These floods may have washed away any surface artifacts that survived the sandy conditions on the terrace and deposited layers of clay and gravel in the areas along its banks. In some places, snail shells have been found in the deposits (Wallace, "1976 Excavations," 1977, 5). Sea level has also changed from the eleventh century to the present, sinking by no more than between one-half and one meter. The higher sea level would place the shoreline closer to the boat-sheds, which at present rest two meters above high tide "measured on a calm summer day with low wave activity" (Henningsmoen 1985d, 351).

Vegetation on the terrace at the time of excavation consisted of subarctic heath and grasses, which flourish in the long hours of daylight in June and July, and vary in

Norse in Newfoundland

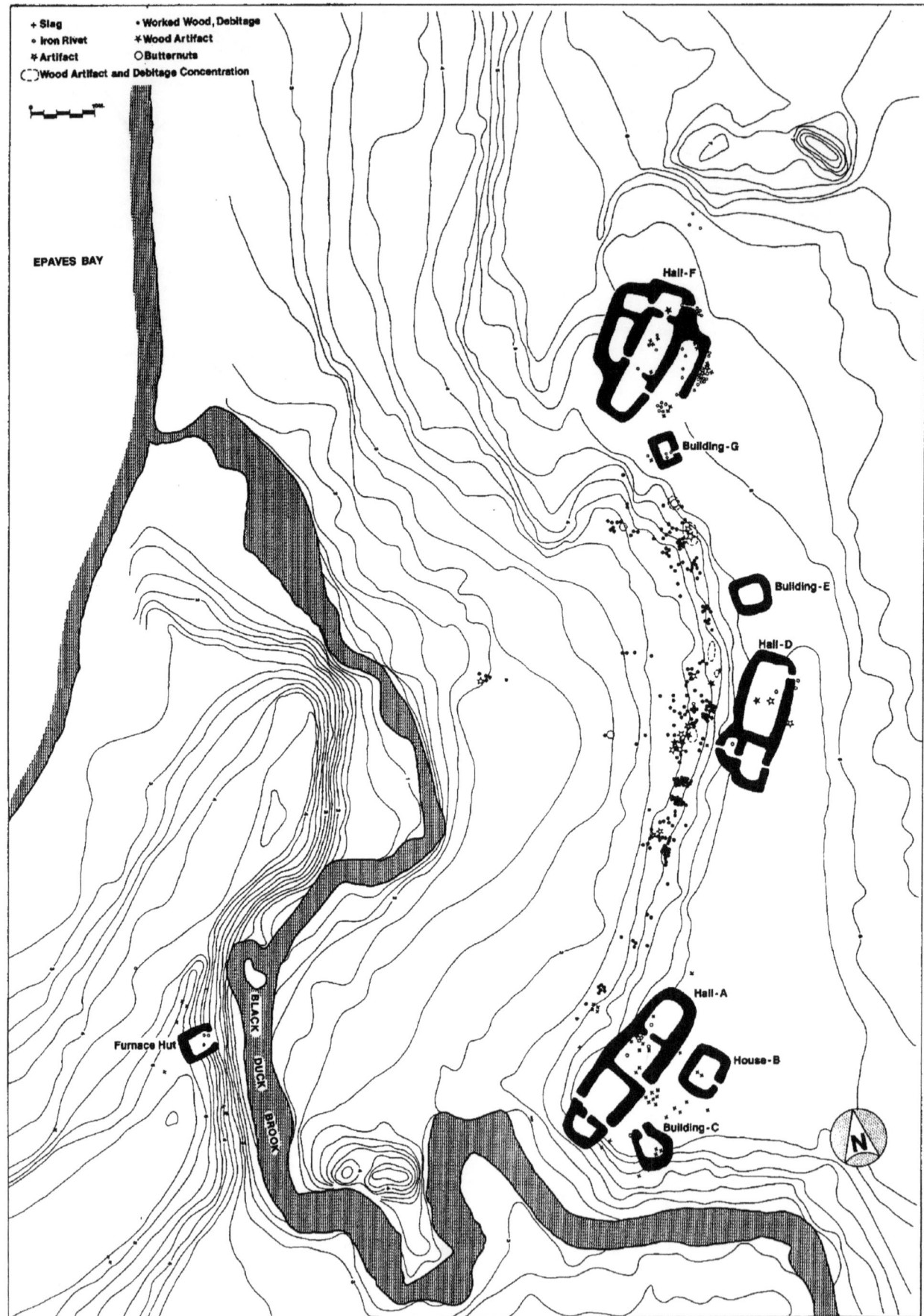

Fig. 2.2b Plan of the site at L'Anse aux Meadows by Wallace (After B. Gallant and B. Wallace in Wallace 1990, 171).

thickness from 2 cm to 15 cm (Schonback et. al. 1976, 8). In the surrounding area dwarf specimens of trees dominated: balsam fir (*Abies balsamea* (L) Mill; tamarack (*Larix laricina* (Du Roi) K. Koch); birch (*Betula sp.*); and willow (*Salix sp.*) (Wallace 1977, "Norse," 4). During the summer, in the bog surrounding the site grew abundant quantities of cloudberries, raspberries, blueberries, cranberries, whortleberries, strawberries, cowberries, gooseberries, red and black currants, and squashberries, the last of which are used by local fishermen to make wine (Ingstad 1971, 186).

Building Construction
Excavation revealed that the walls of all the buildings at L'Anse aux Meadows had been constructed in the *strengur* method (Fig. 2.3), the most ancient of turf-construction methods, and one prevalent on Norse sites in the Viking Age (A.S. Ingstad 1985c, 181).

Fig. 2.3, Photo of strengur *technique used in L'Anse aux Meadows reconstructions (Author)*

The buildings differed from traditional 10th and 11th-century construction in their lack of stone foundations beneath the walls. Similar *strengur*-style turf walls in Iceland and Greenland from the Viking Age have a foundation made of large 'sleeper' stones, sometimes in layers, underneath the blocks of sod; some examples in Greenland contained stones between the layers of turf within the walls themselves, while in other places, turf was crammed between layers of stone. Ingstad interpreted the use of turf as the main construction material—rather than driftwood and timber—as a "weighty argument" that all buildings belong not simply to the same cultural grouping, but to the Norse Viking Age; since there "must in all likelihood have been sufficient timber and drift-wood for building" at the time of settlement. Hence, she reasoned that the settlers must have built their houses from turf out of habit and familiarity, and "they must have come from a country whose natural building material was turf" (A.S. Ingstad 1985c, 155). Wallace's calculations necessitate a surface area of 2,900 m^2 for all construction, roughly equal to the entire surface area of the bog (Wallace 1990, 183). As sod develops slowly, a second event of sod-cutting from the bog would not have been possible in the initial stages of settlement.

Complex A-B-C: Archaeological Description
The southernmost building complex on the side of the terrace east of Black Duck Brook comprised Hall A, House B, and Hut C (Fig. 2.4a and 2.4b). Close proximity to the brook caused problems for the archaeological recovery and interpretation of the complex, factors that will be discussed in the examination and analysis of each building.

Hall A (Fig. 2.5) lay to the north of buildings B and C, apparently sheltering the latter two from the wind off of Épaves Bay. The axis of Hall A ran east-west, with the northern side aligned with the periphery of the terrace (A.S. Ingstad 1985b, 36). Internally, it measured 24 m in length and 4–5 m in width at its widest point, and its four rooms are positioned end-to-end along the east-west axis in the manner of a Norse *skáli*. Room II, furthest west, connects to Room I to the east via a doorway, while Room III, east of Room I, connects to Room IV, furthest east, via another doorway; there is no evidence, however, of a connection between the two central rooms, I and III (A.S. Ingstad 1985b, 39–40).

Room I appeared to be the central living quarters for building A, and earned the building's designation as *Hall A*. Measuring 5.5 m long by 4 m wide, it centered on a long hearth in the middle of the floor. This 2.4 m long by 80 cm wide depression lacked a stone setting, but contained copious amounts of ashes and charcoal, under which the sand had been burned red (A.S. Ingstad 1985b, 41). The surrounding floor, into which bits of charcoal had been trod, was sooty and firm. The long walls north and south of the hearth lacked this firm floor, which suggested that traditional Norse earthen benches may have been built here, covered with some other material, as such structures would prevent the floor from being hard-trodden or sooty (A.S. Ingstad 1985b, 41). These benches could have provided sleeping arrangements for 12 people (Wallace 2006, 38).

Within the doorway connecting Room I to Room II was a small midden. It contained a large number of fire-cracked rocks, as well as charred fragments of bone. Room II, on the western end of Hall A, contained three post holes encircling a small hearth, and other holes for posts which

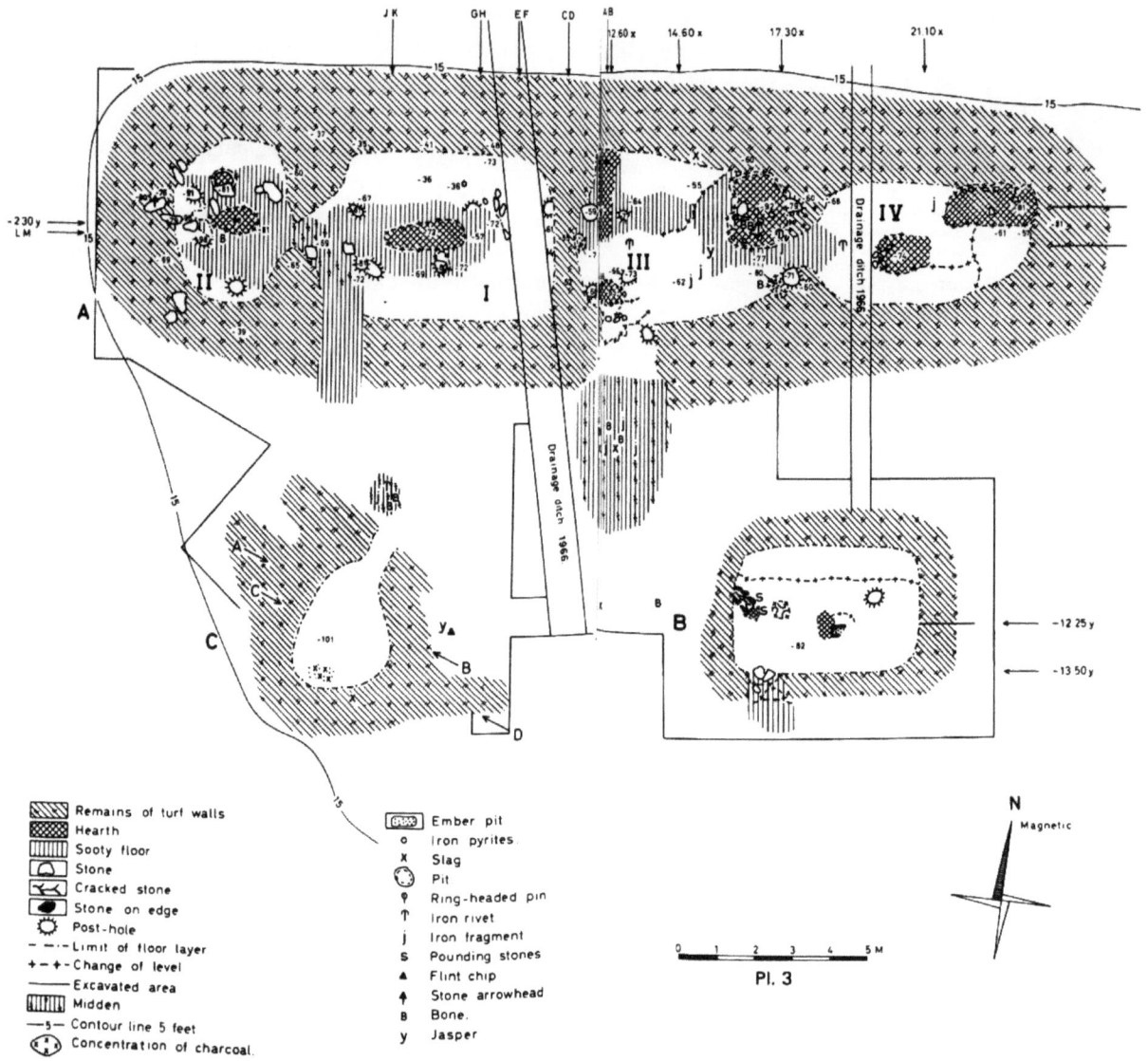

Fig. 2.4a, Plan of Complex A-B-C by Ingstad (After A.S. Ingstad 1985, Pl. 3)

may have supported the roof were found within the room (Fig. 2.6). The room measured 3.3 m by 4 m, and its primary feature—the hearth—measured 1.1 m long by 0.5 m wide with a depth of 10 cm, filled with a mound of fire-cracked rocks, charcoal, and ash, as well as large slabs of slate. This heap of debris rose to the underside of the layer considered to be the collapsed turf roof of the hall (A.S. Ingstad 1985b, 42–3).

Room III seemed to have had no connecting door to the western half of the building. This may be a result of an effort to control the movement of water from Black Duck Brook during its annual spring flooding, an interpretation explored below (Ingstad and Ingstad 2000, 161). Its roof was supported by a series of six posts along the interior perimeter of the room, in contrast to Room I, whose posts stood at a distance from the walls. Room III contained two hearths; the smallest was found in the northwest corner on the northern wall, extending south half-way into the room. This hearth, covered by thick layers of ashes and charcoal, and the floor below it had been burned red, showing up distinctly in contrast with the sooty, hard-trodden main floor (A.S. Ingstad 1985b, 43–5). It contained fragments of bone, several iron nails, and large quantities of smithing slag; a midden outside the eastern entrance to the room also contained a nail, some bone fragments, and slag (Wallace 2006, 39–40).

The main hearth lay in the northeast corner of Room III appeared to have been a large cooking pit, 1.8 m in diameter and 15 cm deep. It contained fire-cracked rocks and charcoal, and had been partly covered by a collapsed

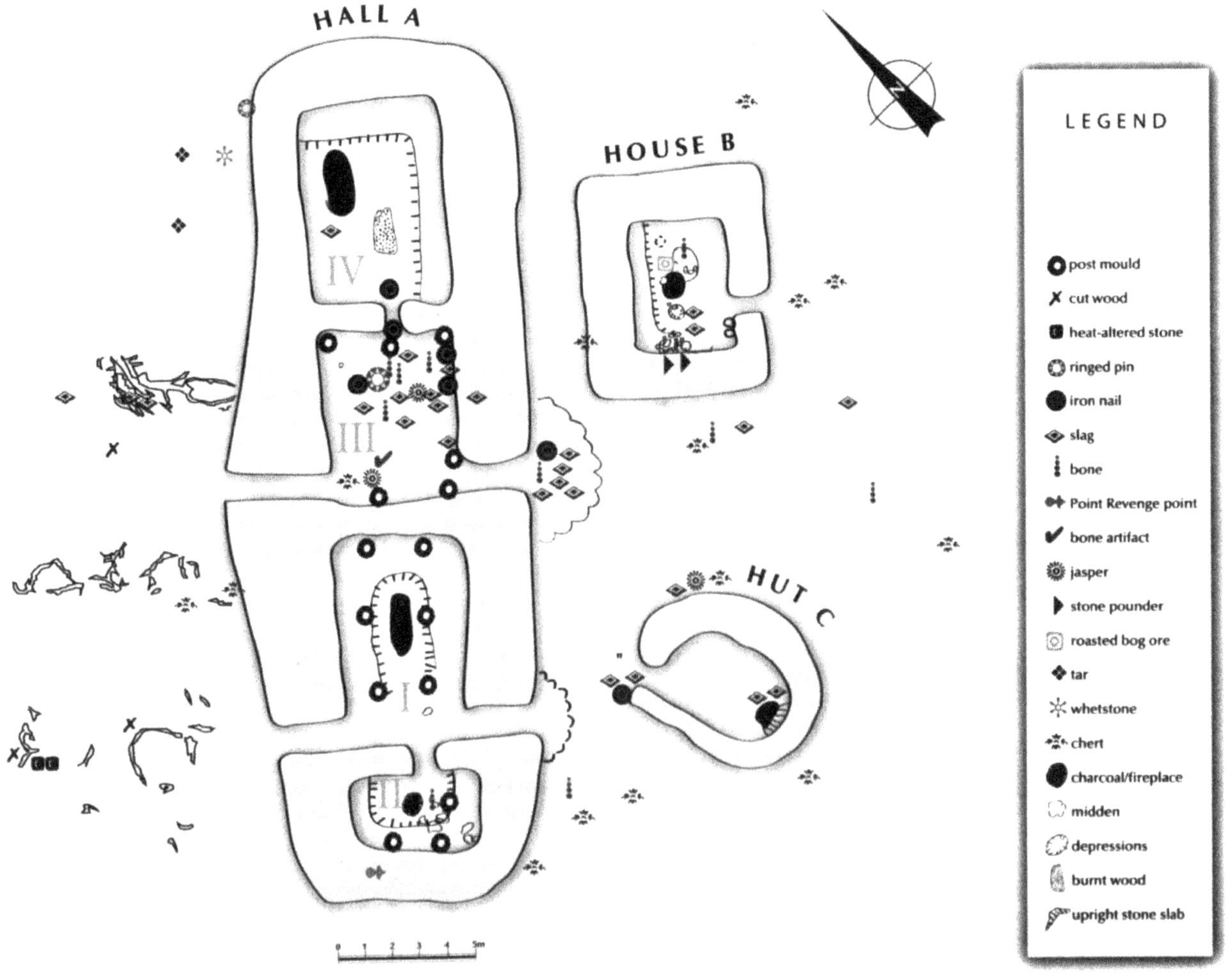

Fig. 2.4b, Plan of Complex A-B-C with artifact placement by Wallace (After Wallace 2006, 39)

Fig. 2.5, Photo of excavated Hall A from the east. (After A.S. Ingstad 1985b, 40)

Fig. 2.6 Photo of post hole in the west end of Room II, Hall A. (After AS.. Ingstad 198b5, 42)

portion of the wall separating Rooms III and IV. In this cooking pit was found a ring-headed pin "indisputably of Norse-Celtic origin," the presence of which, in combination with the housing layout and construction, identified L'Anse aux Meadows as a Norse site (Figs. 2.7 and 2.8) (A.S. Ingstad 1985c, 175). A third fire feature in Room III was a small ember pit in the south-east corner—a depression 50 cm in diameter and 10 cm deep—which was "filled with large, clean pieces of charcoal"; the place where glowing charcoals would have been stored overnight, to aid in starting a fire the next morning (A.S. Ingstad 1985b, 44).

Fig. 2.7, Photo of cooking pit in Room III, Hall A. Post hole to the right of pit. (After A.S. Ingstad 1985b, 43)

Fig. 2.8, Ring-headed pin from Hall A, Room III, length 6.7 cm (After G. Vandervloogt. in Wallace 2006, p. 71)

An entryway connected Room III to Room IV furthest east, which measured 5.65 m long by 3 m wide. Room IV contained two hearths, one in the northeast corner and one in the center of the room. The former was the main cooking pit, 2.4 m long by 90 cm wide at its maximum, and its 15 cm depth consisted of a deposit of fire-cracked rocks, charcoal, and ashes. The central hearth was no more than a shallow depression, 1.1 m in diameter and 6 cm deep, the floor underneath of which was burned red (A.S. Ingstad 1985b, 45). The Parks Canada excavations uncovered evidence of a platform along the eastern and northern walls, based upon the loose earth and loose twigs and other botanical materials along the walls (Wallace 2006, 40).

The western and eastern halves of Hall A differed significantly in layout and composition of hearth structures. The characteristically Norse long hearth in Room I was not found elsewhere in the building, though the slightly smaller hearth in Room II was reminiscent of the long hearth type. Rooms III and IV, in contrast, each had as their main hearth feature a large cooking pit, though each room also contained a smaller, simpler version of the hearths like those in Rooms I and II (A.S. Ingstad 1985c, 164–5). This difference in hearth structure could indicate a difference in occupation between the two halves of the building, also further indicated by the lack of an entryway between east and west.

Another difference between the eastern and western halves of Hall A can be found in the sediment covering the floors and contained within the cooking pits in Rooms III and IV: quantities of light gray charcoal mixed with river sand and gravel. Ingstad interpreted this layer of deposit as silt from the periodic flooding of Black Duck Brook. The presence of this silt in the eastern portion of the hall—the portion farthest from the brook—raised concerns about the contextual stability of the site. Ingstad suggested that the flood water entered the house through the southwestern end of Room III and lingered in Rooms III and IV before receding, removing a great deal of cultural material from the building floor as it exited (A.S. Ingstad 1985b, 323). As the brook flooded each Spring when full of drifting ice, it deposited gravel along the edges and within the A-B-C Complex (A.S. Ingstad 1985b, 37).

The Parks Canada excavations uncovered further evidence of erosion of the turf walls by the brook when they found a thick band of building sod in the bog west of Hall A, between the building and the river. What had once been the western turf wall, and possibly part of the turf roof of Hall A had been washed down the terrace by a Spring flood (Wallace, "1976 Excavations," 1977, 4). The annual flood of Black Duck Brook could also be responsible for the fact that the turf walls of Structures B and C were much thinner than those of Hall A; though Hall A had been disturbed by some of the flood water, Structures B and C received most of its erosive force. Such a force is still present at the site, as shown in Fig. 2.9, a photograph taken upon a visit to the site in June 2010. Such disturbance of context must be taken into account when interpreting the archaeological evidence.

Fig. 2.9, Photo from the east of the space between Hall A and structures B and C, displaying early summer flood (Author)

The one-roomed House B (Figs. 2.10 and 2.12) sat in the southeastern corner of Complex A-B-C, 4 m south of Hall A and east of Hut C. It lay longitudinally parallel to Hall A, measuring internally 4.5–5 m long by 3.25 m wide (A.S. Ingstad 1985b, 46). The entrance was positioned 1 m from the southern wall in the southern corner of the house, marked by a sooty, hard-trodden gap in the wall and by two flat stones; excavation also revealed a depression in the north wall, which may have been a doorway. Along the north wall the firm floor present in the rest of the house was absent, suggesting that a bench had been placed here, an idea confirmed by the excavation of 10 cm of thick layers of black turf along the wall (A.S. Ingstad 1985b, 47). Overall, the Ingstads found much more turf within House B than within Hall A, though its walls were thinner. They concluded that there must therefore have been more sod used in the construction of House B and although the rectangular shape of the house suggested that a supported roof might have been needed, the lack of post holes and abundance of turf could indicate that the roof was built entirely of sod in a corbelled manner, depending on its splayed distribution of weight to remain aloft.

House B contained a surprising number of fire features for its small size: two hearths and an ember pit in its single-roomed building, mimicking the contents of Hall A Room III. The main hearth of House B lay just inside the southern entrance, at the center of the western wall, and could have taken advantage of the draught from the door to release smoke. It consisted of a large stone slab, cracked into pieces, behind a shallow depression 5–6 cm deep of hard, burned sand; the eastern side of the slab was lined by small upright stones (Fig. 2.11) (A.S. Ingstad 1985b, 48). To the east, 20 cm from the main hearth, was the cooking pit, 45 cm in diameter and 25 cm deep. Partially lined with flat stones, it was full of fire-cracked rocks, charcoal, and ashes (Fig. 2.13a and 2.13b).

The third fire feature lay 65 cm further east, roughly in the center of the house. On the left was a 65 cm diameter patch of ash and charcoal 25 cm thick above the floor level, which contained pieces of bog ore, slag, and bone (A.S. Ingstad 1985b, 48; Wallace 2006, 39). To the right was the ember pit, 25 cm wide and 20 cm deep. It was lined with slate and filled with clean charcoal (Fig. 2.14) (A.S. Ingstad 1985b, 48). House B also had turf benches along its western wall (Wallace 2006, 39). House B thus shared several similarities with Hall A in general, and Room III in particular: the turf benches along the wall and the presence of more than one type of fire feature within a room.

Fig. 2.10, Photo of excavated House B from the east, showing the hearths (After A.S. Ingstad 1985b, 49)

Fig. 2.11, Photo of the large hearth in House B. (A. Ingstad 1985b, 50)

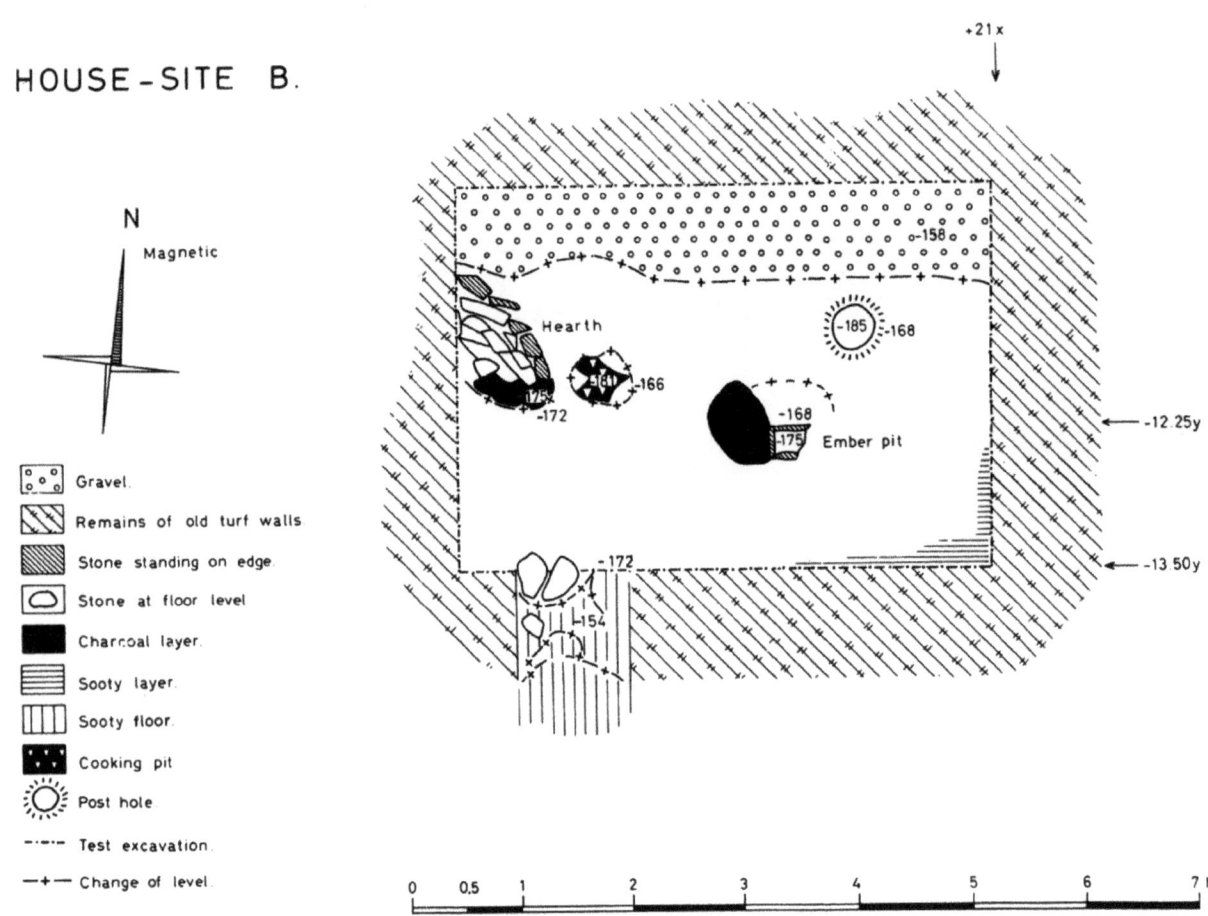

Fig. 2.12, Plan of House B by Ingstad (After A.S. Ingstad 1985, Pl. 13)

Fig. 2.13a, Photo of the cooking pit of House B, with large hearth in back. (After A.S. Ingstad 1985b, 50)

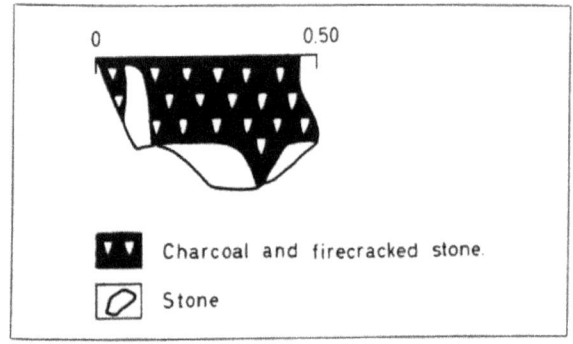

Fig. 2.13b, Profile of cooking Pit in House B. (After A.S. Ingstad 1985b, 52)

Hut C was much cruder in its construction and layout than its adjacent neighbors. Located in the corner of the complex nearest the brook, it was more susceptible to the spring floods. Still, enough of its walls remained to indicate that Hut C was a small, round structure, presumably with a round, corbelled turf roof, such as mentioned above—rather resembling a haystack. This type of small hut is "well-known in the Norse cultural complex," and were commonly used for activities not conducted in the main dwelling (Ingstad and Ingstad 2000, 163). Hut C was small enough to contain only one hearth, though the floor throughout the hut contained charcoal, with its largest concentration around a large stone in the center of the back (southern) wall of the structure, directly opposite the entrance in the northern wall. This stone has been interpreted as the hearth, as it lay on a distinct layer of ten centimeters of earth mixed with charcoal (A.S. Ingstad 1985b, 51). The only other finds of interest in the house were two pieces of slag;

one, located 40 cm high in a turf wall, indicates that Hut C was built after other construction on the site had occurred, as the slag might have been dropped in the turf used to construct Hut C before the sod was cut (A.S. Ingstad 1985c, 191). The midden for Hut C seemed to have been located directly to the north-west outside of the entrance (A.S. Ingstad 1985c, 191). Overall, Hut C was smaller and less complex than Buildings A and B, and its lack of turf benches or any indication of its use as a living space earned its designation as a Hut rather than a House or Hall.

Ingstad argued that the exterior construction of Hut C shows that the inhabitants of Complex A-B-C took precautions to stem the annual floods of Black Duck Brook from erasing their buildings. Excavations uncovered two arms of turf projecting outward from the exterior walls of Hut C: one from the northwest corner towards Hall A, and one from the eastern corner towards Hut C (A.S. Ingstad 1985c, 191). These turf projections "may represent the remains of a turf bank serving as a fence," which in connecting the three houses and fencing in the complex from the southern and western (brook) sides would have prevented the flood waters from washing into the buildings (A.S. Ingstad 1985c, 194). Such measures to control the floodwaters, which wash over the entire part of the terrace on which Complex A-B-C lies, were thus necessary to maintain the structural integrity of the buildings. These turf arms, however, may also have served as a restraining measure for livestock, if any were brought to the site.

Complex A-B-C: Archaeological Analysis
Hall A, with its four rooms joined together in a continuous structure, closely resembles the Iceland *skálar*. Hall A at L'Anse aux Meadows resembled the Icelandic *skálar* and the houses at Jarlshof and Narssaq. All three consisted of several rooms lying in a connected row as one long, rectangular house with walls that bow out slightly. In both houses, the largest room sheltered a long hearth lying lengthwise in the center of the room, though the hearth in Room I of Hall A was less complex than that of Room I in Narssaq, which had a stone edging (A.S. Ingstad 1985c, 164–5). Narssaq, like Hall A, most likely had earthen benches against the side walls along the hearth, as indicated by the absence of a firm floor, and both structures may be designated as *skáli*; though these *skáli* commonly have a roof supported by double rows of posts, as in Room I of Hall A, it was not always universal, particularly in Greenland, where the lack of large trees for timber makes such construction difficult. The farm at Narssaq lacked such a wood-post support for its roof, as did Brattahlið (A.S. Ingstad 1985c, 165).

However, unlike the other houses, Hall A—and indeed the entire site at L'Anse aux Meadows—contained no stone within its turf walls.

Hall A also bore similarities to the Hvalsey complex. The hearth in Room I, in particular, bears a close resemblance to the hearths of Rooms IX and X at Hvalsey; the latter two were of the same simple type as the one at L'Anse aux Meadows, which was a hearth typical of the sort built during the early settlement phase in Greenland. A similar hearth in Room II was also of the same type, though this hearth was covered with layers of stones, clay, and ashes; nevertheless, it has parallels in the farm ruins of Greenland (A.S. Ingstad 1985c, 167). Thus, the layout of Hall A, through comparisons of its structural features, can be shown to be similar to buildings at farm sites in Greenland, though L'Anse aux Meadows itself was not a farming settlement.

Fig. 2.14, Photo of the ember pit in House B. (After A.S. Ingstad 1985b, 52)

House B, a smaller version of Hall A, may also be compared to Room I at Narssaq and Room IX at Hvalsey (A.S. Ingstad 1985c, 188). Additionally, its stone-lined hearth in the north-west corner, placed against a wall, has a particular parallel of that in Room I of the hall at Brattahlið's North Farm (Fig. 2.15) (A.S. Ingstad 1985c, 190); and though Greenland "has few hearths of this type," there are a "considerable number" in Iceland (A.S. Ingstad 1985c, 184). In both Greenland and Iceland, however, where such hearths *are* present, they date to the period of initial settlement (A.S. Ingstad 1985c, 184). Ingstad thus believed it "likely that these two houses [House B and Room I at Brattahlið] should have been built at approximately the same time" (A.S. Ingstad 1985c, 190). House B, as a smaller and contemporary version of Hall A, was most likely built at the same time as Hall A; therefore, if Hall A can be comparatively dated to the early settlement periods of Iceland and Greenland via building construction, and if House B suggests comparisons to other sites built during the same period, it must be concluded that both A and B can be dated via construction comparison to roughly 900–1000 CE, and their source countries may have been Greenland and/or Iceland, by association with Hall A.

Fig. 2.15, Large hearth opposite the door in Room I at the North Farm of Brattahlid (After Nörlund and Stenberger 1934, 58)

Comparisons between the buildings in Complex A-B-C to other Norse North Atlantic outposts can also suggest the roof structure most likely used in Houses B and C; as the flooding of the brook has wiped out evidence of post holes in buildings B and C, comparisons of construction may offer a better answer to the question of roofing than would strict archaeological analysis of the floor level in buildings B and C.

House B, in comparison with the house at Narssaq and Room I in at the North Farm at Brattahlið, may not have had wooden posts to support its roof after all, despite its square structure as mentioned above; neither of those two comparative structures in Greenland showed traces of the rows of posts needed to support such a roof (A.S. Ingstad 1985c, 189–90). Hut C, already suspected of supporting a round roof of turf without wooden beams, has parallels to identical structures in Iceland, where small, round huts known as *fjárborgir* were common. This type of building was constructed entirely of turf, including its corbelled roof, which was built in a domed style, with sod blocks layered so as to decrease the width of the room as the height increased. Reaching the top, a round gap would remain in the center of the roof, which would be commonly covered with a flat stone (A.S. Ingstad 1985c, 193). Though this house was common in Iceland, no doubt it was brought to Greenland by the settlers.

Thus, building construction alone cannot indicate whether the inhabitants of Complex A-B-C—or any individual complex on the site—came from Iceland or Greenland. Though Hall A resembles the house at Narssaq, its *skálar* structure is typical of Iceland. Hearths in buildings A and B are similar in construction and placement to hearths at Hvalsey, Narssaq, and Brattahlid, but these hearth types are also common in Iceland. Hut C is built in a corbelled manner typical of Iceland. Further identification of the home country of the inhabitants of Complex A-B-C will therefore await further information, to be discussed in the next chapter. The one thing which all of the building types mentioned above share, however, is their presence on *early* settlement sites in both Iceland and Greenland.

Complex D-E: Archaeological Description

The second complex on the terrace above Épaves Bay contained two buildings, Hall D and Hut E, and lay north and slightly east of Complex A-B-C (Figs. 2.16a and 2.16b). As before, the close positioning of buildings D and E and their relative distance from the rest of the buildings on the terrace indicate that D and E form a single complex (A.S. Ingstad 1985c, 209).

Hall D lay southwest of Hut E and was oriented along a northeast axis (A.S. Ingstad 1985b, 54). Its external corners were rounded, giving the Hall an oval shape, and its 20 meter exterior consisted of three rooms clustered together, its greatest width 8.7 m; House D was thus the smallest of the halls on the terrace (Wallace 2006, 42). Room I sat in its southern corner, with Room II to the northwest and the large Room III to the northeast. Room II actually lay in front of the terrace, sloping down towards the beach, so that it sat slightly lower than the other two rooms. Room I then connected in the opposite wall to Room II (A.S. Ingstad 1985b, 54). There were three entrances to Hall D, one in the south-eastern wall of Room I, one opposite it in the western wall of Room II, facing the bog, and a possible third in the north-western corner of Room III (Wallace 2006, 43). This last entrance remained hidden during the Ingstad excavations, and was discovered by Parks Canada.

Excavations in Hall D, indeed, "yielded few structural details," thus making the interpretation of construction methods difficult (A.S. Ingstad 1985c, 200). The building walls were built to a thickness of 1.5 m in the *strengur* technique, piling bricks of cut sod atop one another in an interlocking fashion (A.S. Ingstad 1985c, 200), making the support of a turf roof possible. Post hole evidence, however, is limited. Room II had one post hole, while Room III had seven, though not in any discernible prow pattern as would be expected of a Norse *skálar* (Wallace

HOUSE-SITES D AND E.

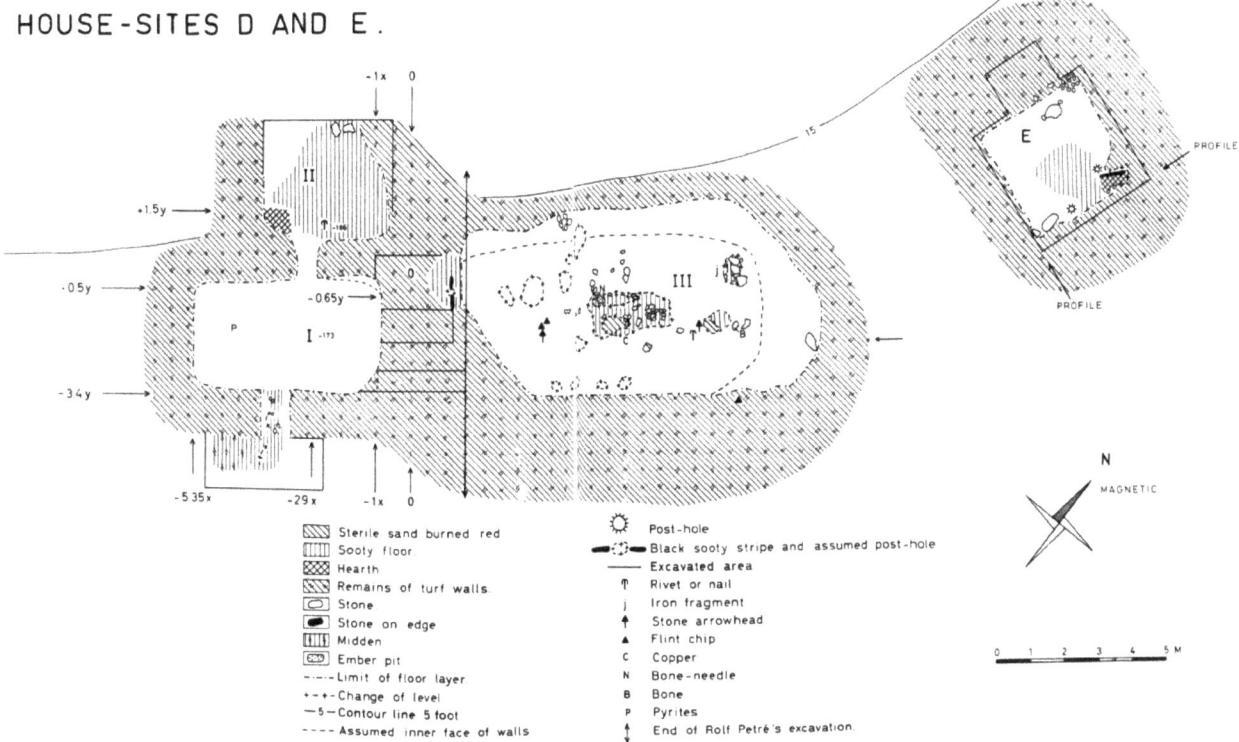

Fig. 2.16a, Plan of Complex D-E by Ingstad (After A.S. Ingstad 1985, Pl. 16)

2006, 43). Anne Stine Ingstad concluded that Rooms I and III may have been jointly roofed, while Room II had its own roof (A.S. Ingstad 1985c, 200); Wallace concluded, however, that each room was roofed independently because of their irregular placement (Wallace 2006, 44).

Room I, measuring 5.5 by 3.2 m, contained no features or artifacts and only shallow cultural deposits; there was, however, a midden directly to the right outside of its entrance in the southwestern wall (Wallace 2006, 44). The entrance was marked only by a hard-trodden and sooty patch of floor on either side of the turf wall, though a stripe in the center of the wall which was not thus worn may indicate a door frame or a threshold. The cultural layer in this room was sparse, containing only a few pieces of charcoal and lacking the large quantities of soot found in other houses on the site (A.S. Ingstad 1985b, 55).

Room II, to the northwest of and on a floor level 30 cm below that of Room I, measured 4 by 3 m. Its profile indicated a strong possibility that a kind of step had been constructed, "reminiscent of those cut out of logs in old Norwegian store-houses" (A.S. Ingstad 1985b, 55). The cultural layer in Room II contained more material than that of Room I, with a 10–15 cm layer of black turf with rust stains and a moderate amount of charcoal (A.S. Ingstad 1985b, 56). Wallace believed that the floor in this room may have actually been covered in wooden planking (Wallace 2006, 44); given the fact that a floor this close to the bog—which was wetter during the Viking Age—would have been difficult to walk on, a wooden floor would be a logical conclusion. In the southern corner, a large fire patch measuring 75 cm in diameter contained a 5 cm thick layer of charcoal (A.S. Ingstad 1985b, 56). Outside of Room II, via the northern entrance facing the bog, the land had accumulated "a great deal of woodworking waste," including "a vast expanse of wood waste along the perimeter of the bog margin" (Wallace 2006, 44).

Room III was the largest in building D, 10 m by 5 m internally, and was designated as a Hall based on its size and central long hearth (Figs. 2.17a and 2.17b). Its construction is puzzling, as there was no evidence of turf walls at one end (Petré 1985, 59); since the two long side walls were barely present, however, the end wall may have simply eroded with time. The northwest side wall, facing the bog, seems to have included gravel in its construction as well, an odd occurrence on this site. The floor consisted of three main layers. The cultural layer, immediately under the grass covering the building, was characteristically loose, comprising a mixture of sand, humus, fire-cracked rocks, slate pieces, a few bones, and a fair amount of charcoal fragments, though it lacked soot. Beneath this layer was one of clean sand and abundant charcoal, much of which was pieces of twig,

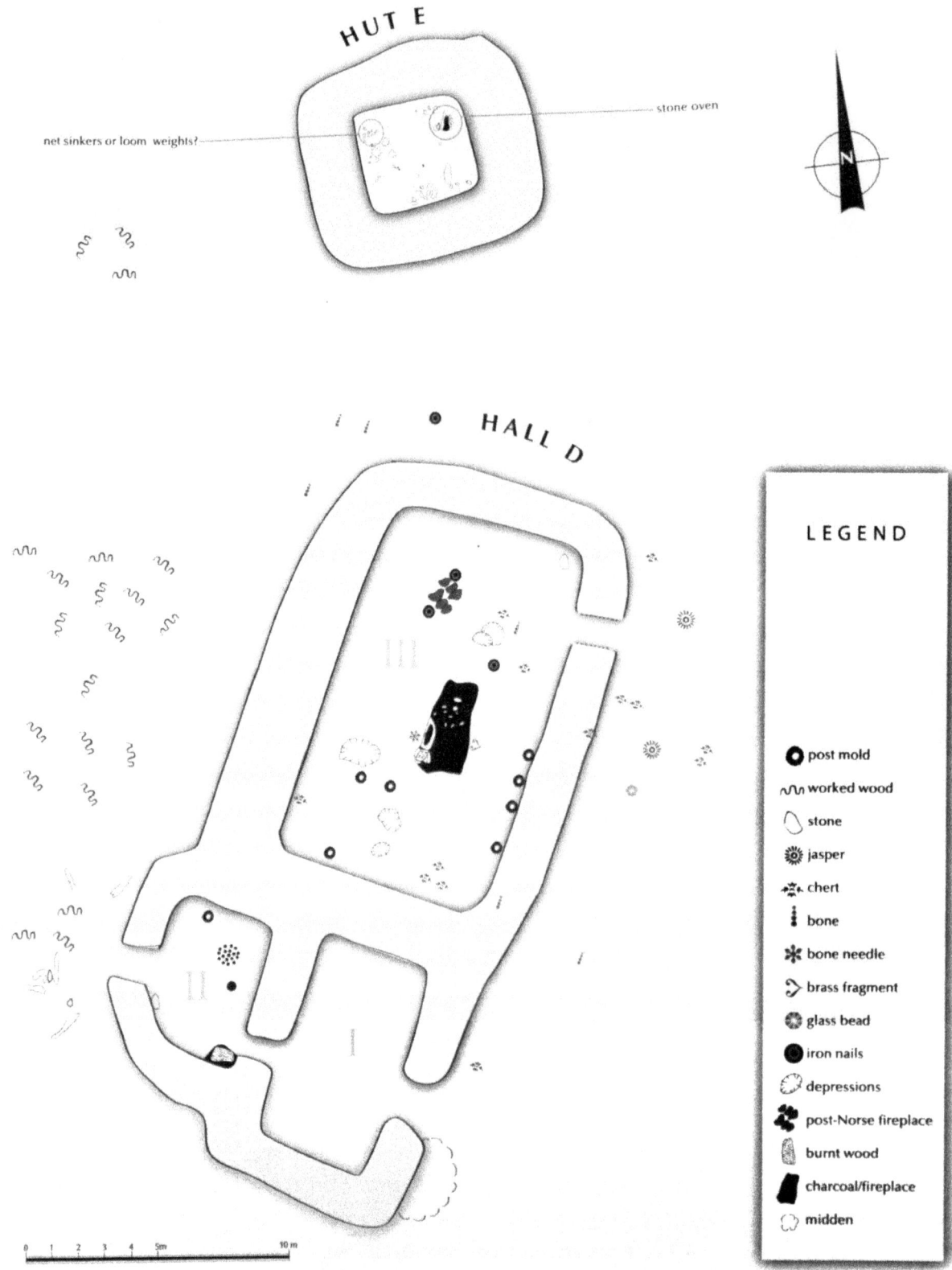

Fig. 2.16b, Plan of Complex D-E with artifact distribution by Wallace. (Wallace 2006, 43)

HOUSE-SITE D III.

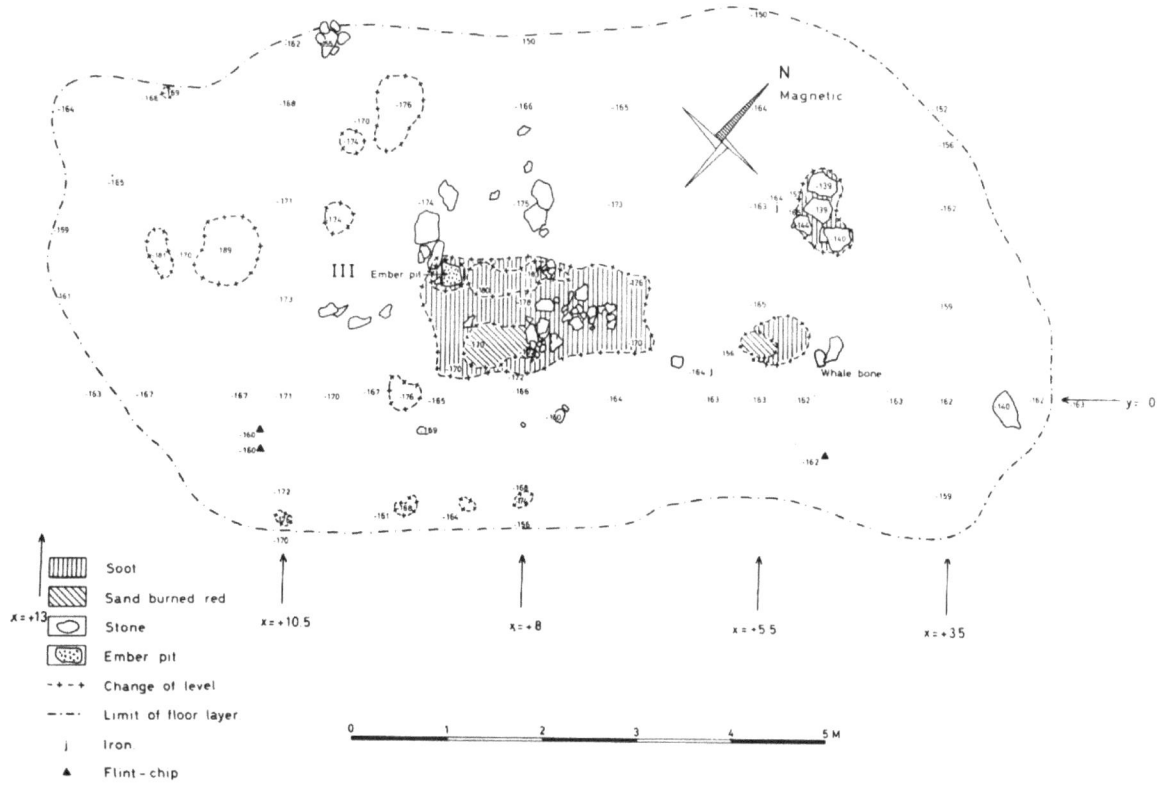

Fig. 2.17a, Plan of Room III, Hall D (After A.S. Ingstad 1985, Pl. 21)

Fig. 2.17b, Photo of Room III, Hall D. (After A.S. Ingstad 1985b, 81)

Room III surrounded a long hearth lying parallel to the length of the building, which was 250 cm long by 100 cm wide, and marked by a layer of soot. Patches of the gravel in this hearth were burned red, as was a depression—1.1 m long by 10–30 cm wide and 5 cm deep—along its north-western edge. Several fire-cracked rocks lay in the north-east corner, and beyond the south-western edge of the hearth was a pit 37 cm by 33 cm and 18 cm deep. In this pit lay a slate slab, next to a similar slab which stood on end in the north-eastern corner of the pit (Petré 1985, 62). The pit, filled with soot and containing no burned sand, "clearly represents the remains of an ember pit of the kind previously encountered here at the settlement" (Fig. 2.18) (Petré 1985, 62).

which suggests the presence of a bedding of twigs or similar material (Petré 1985, 60). Though the floor around the hearth had been compacted, the looser texture of the floor near the edges of the building suggests the areas covered by twigs may have held benches (A.S. Ingstad 1985c, 197). In total, the cultural layer was 30 cm deep. Room III also contained the only trace of interior paneling in Hall D: a stripe of charcoal was found in its southern wall connecting it to Room I (A.S. Ingstad 1985c, 200).

The artifacts present in Hall D need to be mentioned, with further discussion to follow in Chapter 3. In the cultural layer above the hearth in Room III were a number of scattered burnt stones and a small, damaged copper object; this piece of copper may have been used in a belt, as it was covered with cross-stripings. (Ingstad 1971, 183). The ember pit contained fragments of what are considered to be fish bones, as well as a burned, broken bone needle. A large piece of what appeared to be whalebone was found in the area northwest of the hearth

(Petré 1985, 62) in the direction of the possible entrance. Additionally, outside the presumed north-east entrance of Room III was a small glass bead (Fig. 2.19). Flakes and tools of chert and jasper were found near this bead, and chert was also found inside Room III (Wallace 2006, 43).

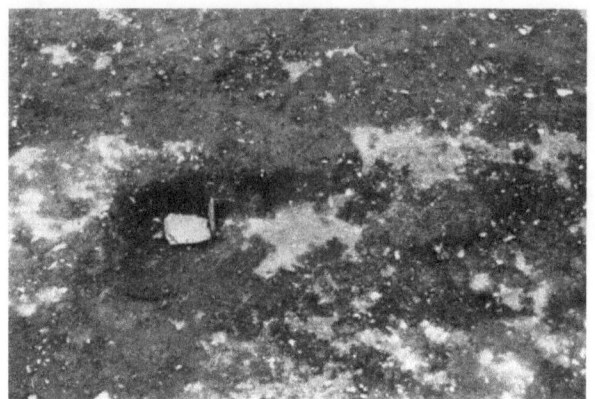

Fig. 2.18, Photo of the long hearth with ember pit in Room III, Hall D. (After A.S. Ingstad 1985b, 81)

Fig 2.19, Glass bead (1.05 cm) from outside the east wall of Hall D, Room III. (After G. Vandervloogt . in Wallace 2006, 71)

Hut E was built 5 m north of Hall D on the terrace, and showed no definitive entrance (Fig. 2.21). Ingstad concluded that the most likely place for an entrance would have been in the southeastern wall, thus facing Hall D and having shelter from the sea; "this is undoubtedly the best and most practical position for an entrance door here in these parts, where the coldest winds blow from seaward" (A.S. Ingstad 1985c, 152). This southeastern position was also the "most common position of doors in the houses on the terrace" (A.S. Ingstad 1985b, 73). Hut E was oriented in the same direction as Hall D, and measured 3.75 m long by 3.25 m wide; and though its external corners are rounded, the interior is rectangular (A.S. Ingstad 1985b, 73). The building was semi-subterranean in a pit-house manner (A.S. Ingstad 1985c, 203). In the northeast corner of the house was a small pile of nineteen fist-sized stones of limestone (A.S. Ingstad 1985b, 76). These stones are an important piece of evidence in the examination of activity at the site, and will be discussed below.

The hearth of Hut E was located in the eastern corner, partly dug under the wall, but lying only slightly below floor level (Fig. 2.20). The floor was hard-trodden to a depth of 10 cm, consisting of sand and soot. The 75 cm by 30 cm hearth "was brim-full of charcoal, ashes, and brittle-burned stone." Its northwest corner was edged by a 75 cm piece of slate, standing on its edge (A.S. Ingstad 1985b, 76). Stratigraphy demonstrated that clean sand had been laid down three times; these layers peeled neatly from one another, and consisted of differentiated layers of clean sand and soot.

About Hut E, Ingstad noted :
"Immediately to the north-west of the slate there was a small depression, 15 cm in diameter and barely 10 cm deep. This may have housed a slender post…No other post holes were found in this house-site…The hole by the south-east wall which we mentioned above may, of course, represent a central post, but it is situated slightly off centre and, moreover, no corresponding post hole was found by the opposite wall" (A.S. Ingstad 1985b, 76)

Fig. 2.20, Photo of hearth in Hut E, with post hole to the left (After A.S.Ingstad 1985, 74)

The post holes near the hearth were recorded on Ingstad's plan of Hut E, but were otherwise unmentioned in further analysis. Ingstad concluded that the manner in which the roof had been constructed could not be determined by the archaeological evidence, but considered it "very likely" that the roof of Hut E had been constructed in the corbelled manner of Hut C (A.S. Ingstad 1985c, 209), which would render post holes useless.

HOUSE-SITE E.

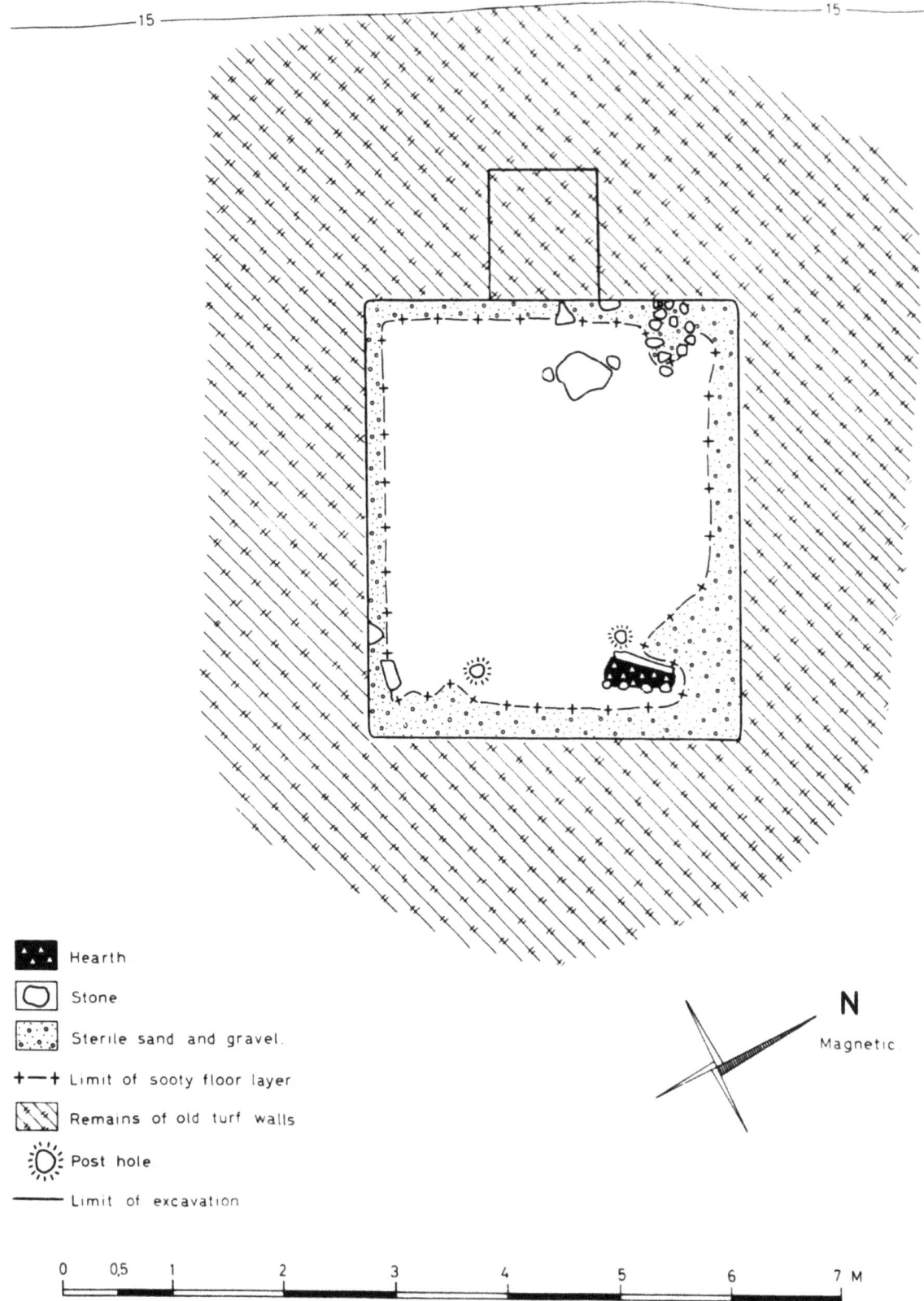

Fig. 2.21, Plan of Hut E by Ingstad, Note the two 'post holes' on either side of the hearth. (After A.S. Ingstad 1985, Pl. 24).

Complex D-E: Archaeological Analysis
At L'Anse aux Meadows, Hall D, Room III, with its long central hearth along the length of the room was "strikingly similar" to Room I of Hall A, Room IX at Hvalsey, and Room I of Narssaq (A.S. Ingstad 1985c, 197). Thus, Hall D followed the typical longhouse pattern, except for the odd placement of Room II, which was added on to the seaward side of Hall D rather than on either end; therefore, Hall D may be compared to either late Icelandic *skáli* or an early Greenland adaptation of the *passage house*, which added one or several rooms onto one end of the longhouse and was characteristic of the later settlements in Iceland; both the longhouse and passage house were used solely as human dwellings, and were surrounded by separate outhouses for work and animal shelter (A.S. Ingstad 1985c, 163).

Hall D, in its resemblance to Hall A, also resembled the longhouse at the North Farm of Brattahlið, the Hvalsey complex, etc. The main hearth in Room III had an almost identical structure as that of room IX at Hvalsey (A.S. Ingstad 1985c, 259). The positioning of Room II perpendicular to the axis of Hall D, however, raised a closer parallel of the Hall to the Stöng house-site in Þjórsárdalur, Iceland. Hall D fits the *Þjórsárdalur-type* model. The evidence in Room III points to it "having been the sleeping hall" (A.S. Ingstad 1985c, 199). Ingstad interpreted Room I as a lobby, there being so few finds and structural details within. The problem in this structural assignment to Hall D lies in the lack of a doorway from Room I to Room III; neither the Ingstad nor Parks Canada excavations uncovered evidence that suggests an interior entrance to Room III, thus its only verifiable entrance remains in the northeastern corner of the house (A.S. Ingstad 1985c, 199; Wallace 2006, 43). Taken alone, Hall D might therefore have been interpreted—as it was by Ingstad—as having internal access between Rooms I and III. Even given the poor preservation conditions at L'Anse aux Meadows, however, the lack of evidence for a doorway in Hall D is best interpreted as the absence of a door connecting the two rooms.

The artifact and feature evidence in Hall D suggested two separate periods of habitation, as excavations revealed two distinct cultural levels. At floor level lay the bone needle, whose drilled eye reveals it to be Norse; such needles are common in the Norse cultural sphere, particularly in Norway and the North Atlantic islands (A.S. Ingstad 1985c, 200). Similarly, the copper found in the ember pit in Room III was chemically revealed to have been smelted, a technique that was unknown in Newfoundland until the arrival of the Norse, who commonly used smelted rather than hammered copper. The two iron rivets found 2 cm above the floor layer in Hall D, near the northeast entrance, resemble most of the iron rivets from the other buildings on the terrace (A.S. Ingstad 1985c, 202). The rivets, therefore, along with the bone needle and smelted copper found at floor level in Hall D, indicated that the initial occupation of the building was Norse. The second occupation, represented by a stratum between 6 to 12 cm above the floor level, contained stone implements, "one of which may be securely identified as representing the Dorset culture" (A.S. Ingstad 1985c, 202); Ingstad concluded that the native Dorset moved into the site at some point after the Norse abandoned it (A.S. Ingstad 1985c, 202).

Hut E, with its sunken floor, resembled a type of house known as *Grubenhäuser*, which was common in Scandinavia (A.S. Ingstad 1985c, 203). These houses were particularly common in western Norway as outbuildings on farms, where they were used as smithies, boatsheds, cowsheds, and fishing huts (A.S. Ingstad 1985c, 206). The relationship between Hut E and Hall D has parallels at a site at Warendorf in Westphalia, where "such sunken-floored huts occur together with longhouses of various shapes and sizes" (A.S. Ingstad 1985c, 208). These small houses differed slightly in structure, some having hearths, and some with timber supports along the walls; in each case, the houses were designed to be used as workspace, and formed complexes with the larger longhouses around them (A.S. Ingstad 1985c, 208).

The method of roof construction at Hut E cannot be conclusively determined; Ingstad found no "securely demonstrable traces of post which might have supported the roof" (A.S. Ingstad 1985c, 206). Based on parallels to Norway and Iceland, it most likely lacked a timber support and was built instead in the same manner of the corbelled roof of Hut C (A.S. Ingstad 1985c, 209). The corner construction of its hearth, particularly the slate slab positioned on edge to protect the hearth from draughts, resembled several other hearths in the buildings on the terrace, as well as many examples from Scandinavia; such corner hearths were particularly common in Greenland, where they "made their first appearance in the sunken-floored huts" (A.S. Ingstad 1985c, 208). Ingstad offered no conclusion as to the significance of the two small post holes along the southern wall of Hut E near the hearth; a building with a corbelled roof would have no need of posts to support a roof. The use of Hut E, however, may be determined based upon more detailed analysis of the positions of features and artifacts in Hut E as compared to similar examples in the Norse cultural complex.

In combination with the heap of nineteen stones found within the hut, the positioning and relative impermanence of the hearth, and the traditional methods of weaving employed by the Norse, the marks in the ground that Ingstad believed to have been left by slender posts could instead be interpreted to have been created by the installation of heavy uprights for a wooden loom, which would have required the nineteen stones as loom weights. The fact that the "post holes" appear to have disappeared by the beginning of Wallace's excavations in the 1970s—as they do not appear on any of Wallace's site plans or in her discussions—suggests that they were not, in fact, post holes, as many of the marks in the other structures that have been conclusively determined to have been left by poles survived beyond the Ingstad excavations to be recorded and discussed by Wallace. Further analysis of these finds will be presented in Chapter 5, but for now it must be mentioned that the extant archaeological information suggests that the two 'post holes' in Hut E were left by a large standing loom.

Icelanders used sunken huts for a variety of purposes, such as cellars or bath houses. Its sunken-floored construction, however, led Ingstad to consider the possibility that it may have been a *dyngja*, an Icelandic sunken-floored house used as women's quarters. These *dyngja*, however, do not typically have hearths (A.S. Ingstad 1985c, 207). Wallace's interpretation, in fact, suggests that Hut E was most likely used for storage or not at all: "Hut E may originally have been envisioned as a pit building, but in this location, the water table is too high for this to be an option" (Wallace 2006, 45).

Complex F-G: Archaeological Description
Furthest north on the terrace above Épaves Bay sits Complex F-G (Fig. 2.22), which was the closest to the bay. Hall F (Fig. 2.23 and 2.24) was the northernmost building at the site, and though it lay roughly the same distance from Black Duck Brook as Complex D-E, it was positioned further back from the edge of the terrace. Hut G sat south of the southern corner of Hall F. Hall F was constructed in the same *strengur* method as the rest of the site, but may have contained some interior wooden construction, "as the great number of charred wooden logs in the cultural layer shows" (Ingstad and Ingstad 2000, 166). The largest building on the terrace, it consisted of six rooms and a shed attached to the eastern wall (Wallace 2006, 45), and measured 20 m long by 15 m wide at its maximum (A.S. Ingstad 1985b, 80).

Entering through the eastern wall of Room I, the northernmost room, one could proceed through the western wall into Room IV or through the southern wall into Room II. From Room II, the western wall led into Room V, while the southern wall continued into Room III. The door in the eastern wall of Room III led back out onto the terrace, directly south of Room VI (the shed), whose southern side showed no evidence of a wall, and whose eastern side held another door. Room VII, south of Room V and west of Room III within the house, lacked evidence of any entrances, though presumably one must have existed (Wallace 2006, 47). Ingstad considered Rooms I, II, and III to have been the central house of the Hall (A.S. Ingstad 1985c, 210–11); based on the sheer size of the building, Ingstad concluded that it was too large to have been covered by one roof, and that Hall F was most likely covered by several separate roofs (A.S. Ingstad 1985c, 210).

Room I measured 4.3 m by 3.45 m internally. It contained two hearths; the first was in the southern corner, between the door to the exterior and the door to Room II, and contained ashes, charcoal, and a pile of fire-cracked rocks. The cultural layer around this first hearth contained much soot and believed by Ingstad to be some type of fat or lard, but did not extend below floor level. The second hearth sat in the middle of the room, consisting of a shallow depression 75 cm long by 50 cm wide and 5 cm deep. It lacked any stone, containing only ashes and charcoal (A.S. Ingstad 1985b, 82). Additionally, Wallace believed that there was probably a platform along the northern wall of the room (Wallace 2006, 45). The sooty, hard-trodden patches of floor that marked doorways in the eastern corner and southern wall lead to Rooms IV and II, respectively; the latter held a depression 1.5 m in diameter and 30 cm deep, which may have once held wooden barrels (A.S. Ingstad 1985c, 220).

Room IV, 3.5 m by 3 m, connected only to Room I (A.S. Ingstad 1985b, 85). The floor contained a large amount of charcoal, and was covered by "several large, charred timbers" (A.S. Ingstad 1985b, 86). Room IV had only one hearth, in the western corner, measuring 1.25 m by 1.20 m, and had two stone chambers, which were separated by a piece of upright slate. A second large, flat piece of upright slate protected the hearth on its

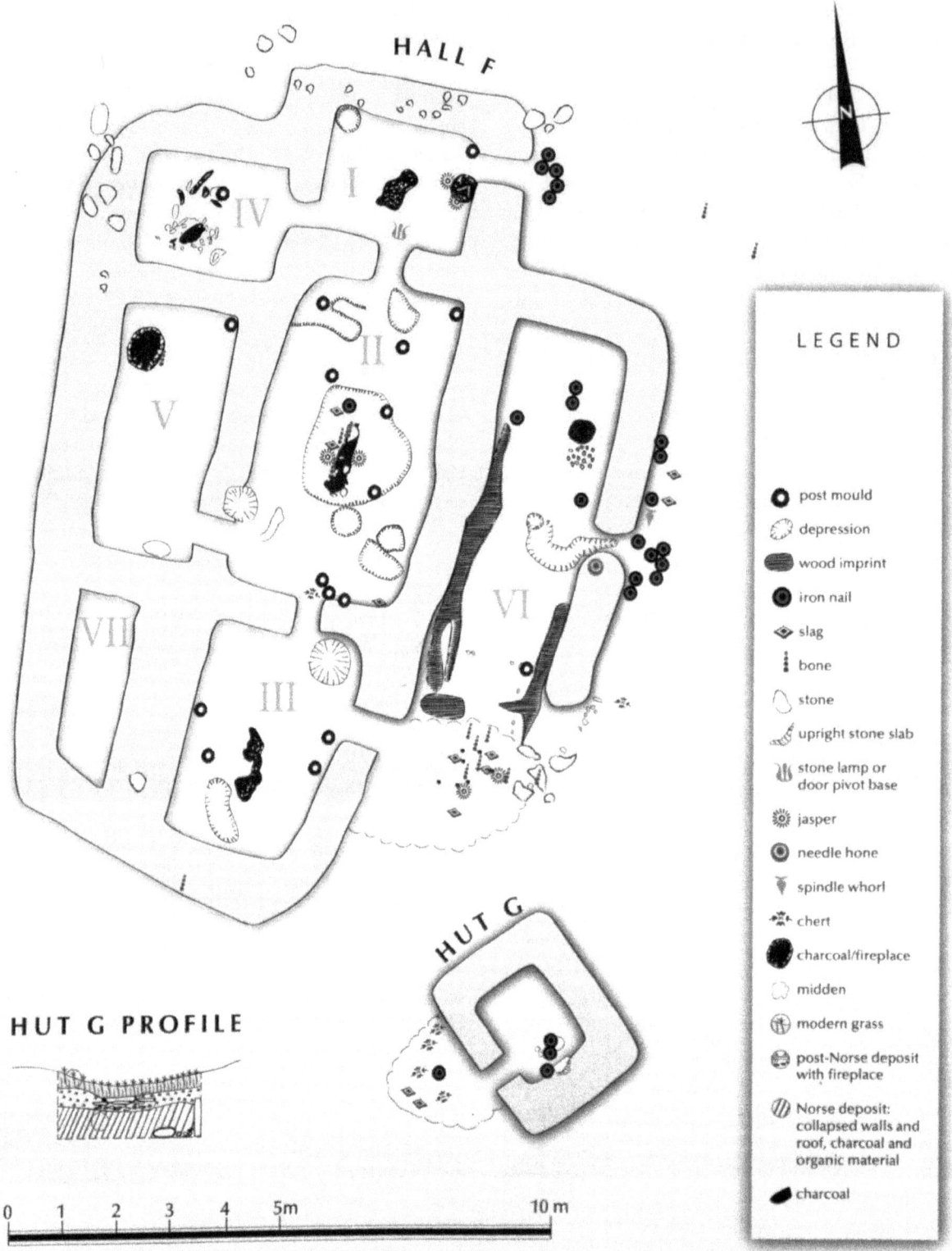

Fig. 2.22, Plan of Complex F-G by Wallace (After Wallace 2006, 47)

northwestern side. Both of the chambers held ashes, charcoal, and pieces of fire-cracked slate (A.S. Ingstad 1985b, 86). One of the chambers may have been used as a stone oven, which could indicated that Room IV may have acted as a separate kitchen (Wallace 1990, 179).

The Parks Canada excavated an additional post hole to the north of this hearth (Wallace 2006, 47), a discovery which will be an important factor in the taphonomy of the site to be discussed in greater detail in Chapter 5.

Complex D-E: Archaeological Analysis

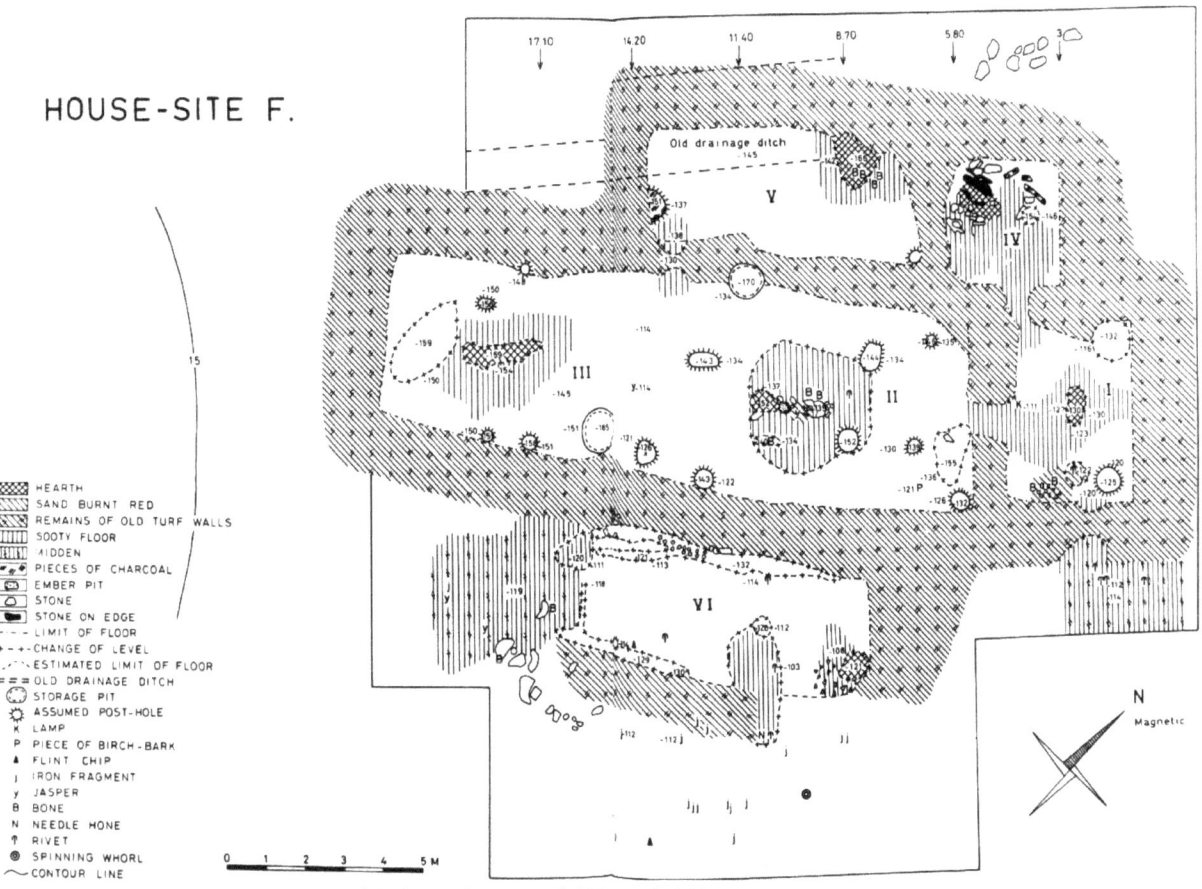

Fig. 2.23, Plan of Hall F by Ingstad (After A.S. Ingstad 1985, Pl. 27)

Fig. 2.24, Photo of Hall F from the northeast. (After A.S. Ingstad 1985, 77)

Room II contained one hearth, 1.9 m long by 40–50 cm wide and 40 cm high, which ran parallel to the length of the house in the center of the room; its southwestern end was a cooking pit, 50 cm in diameter and 15 cm deep, full of fire-cracked rocks, ashes, and charcoal (Fig. 2.25a and 2.25b). The northeastern edge of the long hearth was delineated by a large, flat, fire-cracked rock. Surrounding the entire hearth, the firm floor contained substantial amounts of soot and charcoal, as well as many small stones and several fragments of burned bone. The floor became considerably less compact along the side walls of the room, for a width of 1.5 m which was "somewhat higher than the floor around the hearth" (A.S. Ingstad 1985b, 84). Ingstad concluded that the areas of looser earth may have lain beneath raised benches most likely made of wood, as the sand matrix contained "a large number of fairly large pieces of charcoal" (A.S. Ingstad 1985b, 84). Directly north of the cooking pit was another fire feature, lined with stone on the bottom and along its sides, 25 cm long and 10 cm high (Fig. 2.26). Ingstad interpreted this as an ember pit "of the same type as those encountered in house B and in D III" (A.S. Ingstad 1985b, 83). Within Room II, Wallace confirmed Ingstad's excavation of nine post holes, placed at odd intervals throughout the room; four are distributed evenly throughout the northern half of the room, two are contained within the depression surrounding the hearth, and three are tightly clustered on the eastern side of the doorway into Room III (Wallace 2006, 47).

Room II measured roughly 4 m by 10 m; it may have with Room III formed one large room with Room III, or have had a wall of which no archaeological trace remains. The area presumed to be Room III, however, lies slightly lower than Room II, suggesting that the two were separate. The separation of the hearths into two distinct features rather than one longer hearth, which could straddle Rooms II and III, also suggested that there were indeed two rooms.

Room III measured 9 m long by 4–5 m wide (A.S. Ingstad 1985b, 83). Its cultural layer was 25 cm deep, consisting of three distinct layers. The turf over the house held three large stones above the hearth below, indicating a smoke opening in the roof, beneath which the second layer contained a large quantity of embers. The hearth was in the center of the room, a depression 1.8 m long by 40 cm wide which lacked any kind of stone setting or artifact evidence beyond charcoal (A.S. Ingstad 1985b, 85). Room III had four post holes, two on either side of the hearth, relatively close to the walls, and arranged opposite one another (Wallace 2006, 47), but had no "securely demonstrated" benches along the walls (A.S. Ingstad 1985b, 211). There was an entrance from the exterior of the hall to Room III, in its southeast corner, which may have incorporated a door or threshold. Outside of this door lay a wide midden, similar in accumulation to the cultural layer of an interior room (A.S. Ingstad 1985b, 80).

From the northwestern wall of Room II, a 'door' in the partition led into Room V, "merely marked by a hard-trodden depression going some way into the

Fig. 2.25a, Long hearth with cooking pit, ember pit, and flat stone in Room II, Hall F. (After A.S. Ingstad 1985b, 81)

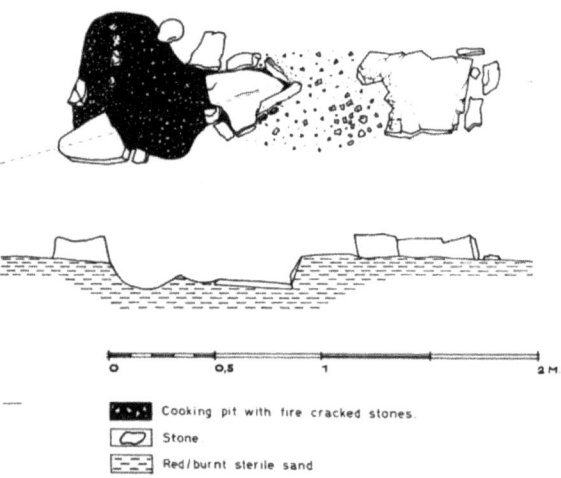

Fig. 2.25b Plan and section of hearth in Room II, Hall F. (After A.S. Ingstad 1985b, 84)

Fig. 2.26, Photo of ember pit of the long hearth in Room II, Hall F. (After A.S. Ingstad 1985b, 83)

wall on both sides, with a sterile central part" (A.S. Ingstad 1985b, 87). After removal of the turf wall that had collapsed into the room, a single hearth was exposed, in the northeastern corner; it measured 55 cm deep and 1.1 m in diameter. It contained not only fire-cracked rock, ashes, and charcoal, but also a few fragments of burnt bone. The cultural layers above and below this hearth had a consistency like that of fat, and in the rest of the room the cultural layer "was in the nature of a thick burned stratum containing large, dry pieces of charcoal and charred timbers" (A.S. Ingstad 1985b, 88). A second feature, a 50–75 cm diameter pit along the southern wall, was filled to its 20 cm depth with pure charcoal; though it resembled an ember pit, such a fire feature would have lain much closer to the hearth than this pit did. Thus, Ingstad concluded that it most likely is the remains of a post which burned within its post hole (A.S. Ingstad 1985b, 88); a second post-hole in the northeastern corner makes this explanation plausible.

Along the western wall of Room V Ingstad found a ditch filled with stones and gravel; a meter and a half wide and 60 cm deep, it ran through the room and leads both to Room IV in the northeast, and to what Wallace would later discover to be a seventh room in the southwest. Ingstad interpreted this ditch as a drainage measure "dug for the purpose of leading away the melting snow from the hillock north-west of the house" (A.S. Ingstad 1985b, 88). Had livestock been brought to L'Anse aux Meadows and kept inside Hall F, the drain could have served as a byre; there is no archeological evidence, however, of livestock having been kept in this structure; the usual entomological and macrobotanical evidence of livestock and their feed are not present. This feature raises more questions than it answers. Room VII, discovered in 1975, showed no feature or artifact evidence and is the same width as Room V and length as Room III.

Fig. 2.27, Photo of Room VI, Hall F, from the southwest, showing wooden impressions in floor. (After A.S. Ingstad 1985b, 90)

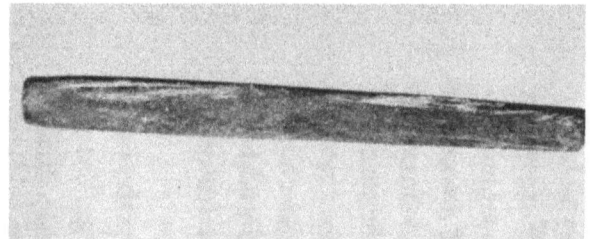

Fig. 2.28, Needle hone from Hall F, Room VI, 7.3 cm long by 0.7 cm section (After A.S. Ingstad 1985b, 91)

Room VI, on the eastern side of the Hall, was more of a shed than a true room, having neither a southern wall made of turf nor a floor surface (Wallace 2006, 46); it also lacked a door into the interior of thebuilding. Its internal measures are 3.2 m wide by 8 m long. The eastern and northern walls of this room were made of turf, and though no remains of a southern wall were found, it may have been made of wood, "as the narrow groove at the south-western end of the floor would seem to indicate" (A.S. Ingstad 1985b, 89); such construction was confirmed by the presence of channels running along the interior of the side walls in the southern half of the room, which were filled with decayed wood, and likely once held paneled walls (Fig 2.27) (A.S. Ingstad 1985c, 214). Additionally, the fact that the north edge of the midden—outside of the exterior entrance to Room III, south of Room VI—stopped at the southern limit of the eastern turf wall of Room VI suggested that there was indeed once a wall here.

Only one hearth was present in Room VI, in the north-eastern corner north of the entrance. Under the large, flat stone that covered it lay fire-cracked rocks, ashes, and charcoal, and around the hearth lay five small lumps of corroded iron interpreted by Ingstad as slag (A.S. Ingstad 1985b, 92), which upon metallurgical analysis Wallace later discovered to have been nails (Wallace 2006, 47).

Most of the artifact evidence for Hall F came from Room VI (A.S. Ingstad 1985b, 92), though some came from the hearth of Room II, which contained slag and bone fragments. Room VI and its environs, however, had the majority of the finds. The outdoor midden between rooms III and VI contained bone fragments, iron slag, and pieces of jasper. Within Room VI, near the northeastern entrance, was a needle hone made of quartzite (Fig. 2.28). Outside the entrance lay pieces of slag and a number of iron nails (Wallace 2006, 47); Wallace believed that their placement outside the room was a result of post-depositional processes, and that they originally lay within Room VI (Wallace 2006, 48). Of the 99 fragments of iron nails found at L'Anse aux Meadows, 78 came from Complex F-G, and 60 percent of those from Hall F Room VI (Wallace 2000c, 211). Also found outside Hall F by its eastern wall was a spindle whorl made of soapstone (see Chapter 3).

Throughout Hall F, similarities in the excavated cultural layers necessitated examination. Under the grass covering the ruins was a coal-black layer that contained a considerable amount of charcoal, as well as a number of stones; beneath this lay a 10 cm layer of turf, presumably the original roof of the structure. The layer below the roof also contained a great quantity of charcoal, but was looser in consistency, and was mixed with sand. The actual floor, beneath this looser third layer, still contained charcoal, but had "a consistency rather like that of cheese" (A.S. Ingstad 1985b, 79), and it was in this layer that most of the finds and the burned fragments of bone lay. The soil beneath the cultural layer had been burned red. Except for Rooms III and VI, these conditions were present throughout the hall. Ingstad thus concluded that the house "had been ravaged by fire, but this [fire] had obviously not raged equally severely throughout" (A.S. Ingstad 1985b, 79). The lack of fire in Room III may in fact aid in arguing for the presence of a wall between Rooms II and III, "so that the fire was either stopped by the wall, or burned itself out while ravaging the wall" (A.S. Ingstad 1985b, 85).

Hut G (Fig. 2.29), five meters to the south of Rooms VII and III of Hall F, measured almost 2 m^2 (Fig. 2.25a and 2.25b). Rather than having been constructed out of turf, it was dug into front of the raised terrace, thus having four gravel walls; since its construction, the northwestern wall facing the sea had eroded, and it is possible that this eroded wall may have originally included a door (A.S. Ingstad 1985b, 93). The one-room structure contained three large stones above the cultural layer—two stacked atop a flat slate—which lay on top of 60 cm of charcoal and sand, and were most likely used as coverings for a smoke hole in the roof of the house. The hearth for Hut G sat against the southwest wall, which was protected from draughts by a stone slab, upright and cracked by fire. In front of it was a layer of charcoal containing fist-sized fire-cracked rocks; "the great number of brittle-burned stones the size of a clenched fist and larger are characteristic of the cultural layer of this small house" (A.S. Ingstad 1985b, 95). Amongst the rocks, and in the midden outside the entrance, were iron nails; the midden also contained small pieces of slag. The floor of Hut G—10 cm thick—was blackened by soot and very compact. Near the hearth also lay a large stone, for which there is no explanation (A.S. Ingstad 1985b, 94).

Complex F-G: Archaeological Analysis
Hall F resembled Halls A and D in its construction, a modified longhouse type. Hall F, however, lacked the pairs of post holes along the middle of the floor that are found in the typical longhouse (A.S. Ingstad 1985c, 212). Its long hearths in Rooms II and III and earthen benches in Room II were, like those in Halls A and D, similar to those at Narssaq and Hvalsey (A.S. Ingstad 1985c, 211); "when assessing the cultural complex here represented, the hearths of house F, which are of four different types, are of particular importance" (A.S. Ingstad 1985c, 215). Wallace believed that Hall F, as the largest building on site, was "most likely where the leader of the settlement resided with his personal crew" (2006, 45).

Hall F, with its seven rooms and sod structure, resembled both Icelandic and Greenland buildings from the eleventh and twelfth centuries (Schonback et. al. 1976, 8). It had Icelandic as well as Greenland types of hearths (A.S. Ingstad 1985d: 260). The hearth in Room II was of the Greenland type (A.S. Ingstad 1985c, 213), and as Helge Ingstad emphasized, the hearth in Hall F was of a similar type as that "in the so-called Fireplace Area in the homefield of Brattahlið in Greenland, the farm of Eirik the Red and Leif Eriksson!" (Ingstad and Ingstad 2000, 148).

Ingstad believed the *Þjórsárdalur-type* to provide "the closest parallels for house F" (A.S. Ingstad 1985c, 210), as Hall F comprised a main house of several rooms aligned in a row, with additional rooms built onto the side; the construction of Room VI on the eastern side contradicts this parallel, but Ingstad explained this as an adaptation to this site, as "such a room would lie in the sun at the same time as it would be protected from the cold winds from the sea" (A.S. Ingstad 1985c, 210). The post holes of Hall F, however, are not arranged in pairs of rows like the Icelandic *skáli*, but rather lack a defined pattern, in a manner similar to the centralized houses of contemporary Greenland. Similarly, the conglomerate construction of Hall F, in contrast to the Icelandic *Þjórsárdalúr type*, resembles more closely the Greenland centralized house, with its seven rooms clustered tightly together rather than arranged in a long line with one or two rooms branching off.

Building construction evidence for Hall F, unlike Halls A and D, seems to point to an origin for its inhabitants in Greenland; not only is its layout typical of early Greenland settlement, but its hearths and benches are similar to those found at Narssaq and Hvalsey (A.S. Ingstad 1985c, 211). Part of the difficulty of interpreting the remains of Hall F is the fact that Room VII was not discovered until the later Parks Canada excavations; it was not found by the Ingstads, and was therefore not included in their analysis (Wallace 2006, 46).

The "drainage ditch" which Ingstad excavated in Room V leading to Room VI presents an interesting puzzle. On any other Norse site, the presence of gravel and stone in a linear fashion so close to a wall would suggest a stone foundation to the turf wall; at L'Anse aux Meadows, however, where none of the walls have stone foundations, the 'drainage ditch' suggests several possibilities. The first is that it was, in fact, a drainage ditch: however, there was no evidence of livestock being kept in any of Rooms IV, V, or VII, so there was no definite need for internal drainage. If the drain was to keep rainwater away from the building, then why would the inhabitants place the drain underneath the building itself? The second possibility is that there was stone within this northwestern wall of Hall F, in which case the questions is raised as to why stone would be used in only one wall of the entire site? This drainage ditch, however, is one of the two archaeological features on the site which could suggest that livestock may have been kept at L'Anse aux Meadows, the second being the arms of turf projected from Complex A-B-C.

A third possibility is that this drainage system worked as a sort of internal plumbing, as seen in relation to several contemporary farm buildings in Greenland. A similar drain and well system was found in the Hall at Narssaq (Albrethson 2000, 98–9), and also in Room VI of the North Farm at Brattahlið. The well at Brattahlið was not simply a pit dug down into the ground, but rather the result of the running of a small stream through a stone conduit in the wall. The water collected in two basins before flowing through another conduit out of the well and

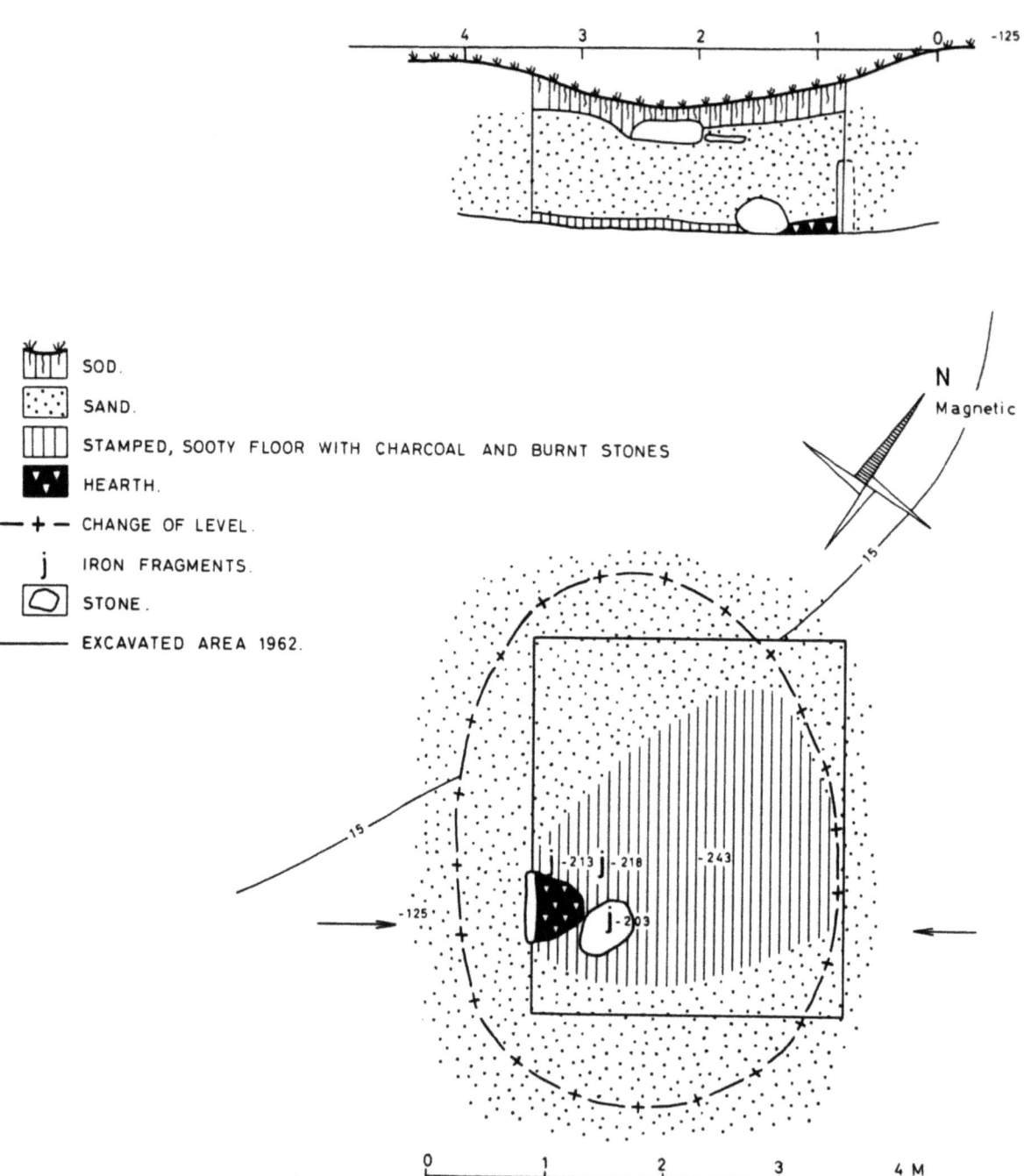

Fig. 2.29, Plan and section of House G by Ingstad. (After A.S. Ingstad 1985, Pl. 36)

onto the midden outside (Nörlund and Stenberger 1934, 68). In light of this comparative evidence, the stone "drainage ditch" in Hall F at L'Anse aux Meadows may have functioned in a similar way to redirect water from the outside of the building into the hall, in order to provide running water to its inhabitants.

Hut G showed no direct evidence of its particular use, but the hearth and the large quantity of fire-cracked rocks in the cultural layer indicated that "big fires must have been lit here" (A.S. Ingstad 1985c, 237). One possible explanation is that this building was used as a bath-house, or sauna, several of which are known in Greenland, and to which Hut G has several similarities: size, shape, construction, and artifact assemblage (Ingstad 1971, 183); a typical Norse bath-house usually "had a stone stove and loose stones which were heated before bathing; then cold water was poured on the stones, quickly producing steam" (A.S. Ingstad 1985c, 237). In the West Settlement of Greenland at Umíviarsuk, one of the ruins was identified as a bath-house; in it was a stove for heating rocks and a wooden platform for sitting upon. The parallel to Hut G was in the "remarkably great number of brittle-burned stones" found within the house at Umíviarsuk (A.S. Ingstad 1985c, 239). If, as seems possible, Hut G was a sauna, the slate slab atop the roof would have covered the smoke hole and contained the steam (A.S. Ingstad 1985c, 237). Additionally, identifying the structure as a sauna accounts for the presence of Feature 7, a drain which ran down the slope southeast of Hut G; one would need water to produce steam, which could be brought by a drain from the peat bog behind Complex F-G at a higher elevation (A.S. Ingstad 1985c, 239).

The Smithy (Building J): Archaeological Description and Analysis
Across Black Duck Brook from the main terrace, the remains of a final building sat above the bay in isolation. This structure has been identified as the Smithy on the basis of its construction, location, and the large amounts of slag and charcoal which it contained (Fig. 2.31a and 2.31b).

The building was first identified as a 2.75 m by 3.75 m long depression in the bank of the brook (Fig. 2.30a and 2.30b) (Eldjárn 1985, 98). Immediately below the sod covering of the ruin Ingstad's team found a layer of sand mixed with charcoal and some pieces of slag (Eldjárn 1985, 97). The cultural layer was 25–30 cm deep, distributed evenly amidst the depression, and contained large amounts of charcoal and crumbled charcoal mixed into the sand, along with alternating patches of pure sand and charcoal (Eldjárn 1985, 98). Also present in this cultural layer was a considerable amount of slag—ranging in size from very small bits to pieces the size of an egg—and "lumps of a white, clay-like material, some of them apparently glazed on one side" (Eldjárn 1985, 100); conspicuously absent was evidence suggesting that the building had been "a house with walls and a roof" (Eldjárn 1985, 99).

Fig. 2.30a, Photo of Smithy seen from the river, with the charcoal kiln in the back left. (After Eldjárn 1985, 97)

Fig. 2.30b, Photo of Smithy prior to Parks Canada excavations, 1975. (After Wallace 2006, p. 61)

In the southeast corner of the structure lay a large flat, horizontal stone anchored firmly in the floor, from which it extended 8 cm. Though broken at one end, the stone had obviously once been rectangular; this stone was interpreted as the anvil (Fig. 2.32) (Eldjárn 1985, 101). Around this large stone were small slivers of stone, which appeared to come from the larger stone, and a layer of white clay, which must have been placed intentionally as a setting for the anvil. The stone faced a round hollow in the smithing floor, the bottom of which contained a layer of crumbled charcoal and slag 2 cm deep; "the stone was the anvil and the fireplace the forge" (Ingstad 1971, 190). North of the hollow, towards the entrance to the, lay the highest concentration of slag, while behind the stone charcoal predominated, in layers up to 8–10 cm thick in the rear part of the building depression (Eldjárn 1985, 101).

Fig. 2.31a, Plan of Smithy by Eldjárn (After A.S. Ingstad 1985, Pl. 39)

Fig. 2.32, Stone anvil in Smithy (After Eldjárn 1985, 100)

The use of building J as a smithy can be confirmed by the high concentration of slag and charcoal found in it, as well as by its positioning on the site relative to the other structures. The presence of a smithy at L'Anse aux Meadows is not unusual, as Norse complexes often had their own smithies; they typically placed smithies "away from the dwelling houses, because of the danger of fire, and often on the bank of a river" (A.S. Ingstad 1985c, 235). Cultural comparisons for the smithy can be found at Keldur, the oldest farm in Iceland (Ingstad and Ingstad 2000, 165), as well as at Gjáskógar in Iceland (Wallace 2000c, 211). A similar building, determined to be a smithy, was found at Jarlshof. The one-room building (House 1B) had an open hearth of "four large stones roughly set in the centre of the floor," one of which was used as an anvil. The cultural layer above this hearth consisted of 5 cm of peat ash containing 52 iron fragments (Hamilton 1956, 111). In total, over 135 pieces of iron or iron slag were found at Jarlshof, which were primarily interpreted as "clinker nails used in the repair or construction of boats" (Hamilton 1956, 116).

Charcoal Kiln and Cooking Pits: Archaeological Description and Analysis

Southwest of the Smithy on the terrace was a feature nearly two meters in diameter, identified as a charcoal kiln by a 70 cm aggregation of charcoal layers (Ingstad 1971, 190). The lowest layers contained pure charcoal, while increasing amounts of sand were mixed with the charcoal towards the top of the pit (Eldjárn 1985, 103–4). This kiln was necessary to create the large amounts of charcoal needed for the extraction of usable iron from bog ore. Placed below ground, the kiln would have been protected from the draughts off of Épaves Bay (A.S. Ingstad 1985c, 240–1).

Two cooking pits were found on the site. Cooking Pit I was also on the west side of Black Duck Brook, 45 m northeast from the Smithy, an oblong depression parallel with the shore and which had been dug into the gravel bank (Eldjárn 1985, 106). Measuring 2.3 m long by 1.1 m wide at the top, it narrowed to a length of 1.7 m at its lowest depth of 70 cm (Fig. 2.33a and 2.33b). The bottom layer of the pit was a thick (4–15 cm) layer of charcoal, which rises up the sides of the pit. Above this charcoal was a partially differentiated layer of reddish burnt sand which contained some small pieces of turf. At the top was a thick layer of stones in a range of sizes; some were small shore-pebbles, but most were roughly the size of a clenched fist. There were no artifacts within or near this pit, however, and it was interpreted as a cooking pit, "where meat was cooked on glowing embers and heated stones" (Eldjárn 1985, 107). This typical Scandinavian fire-feature is called a *seyðir*, a type of outdoor oven, in which the meat was surrounded and covered with hot earth and stones to cook. Examples have been found in excavations in Iceland (Shetelig and Falk 1978, 310).

Complex D-E: Archaeological Analysis

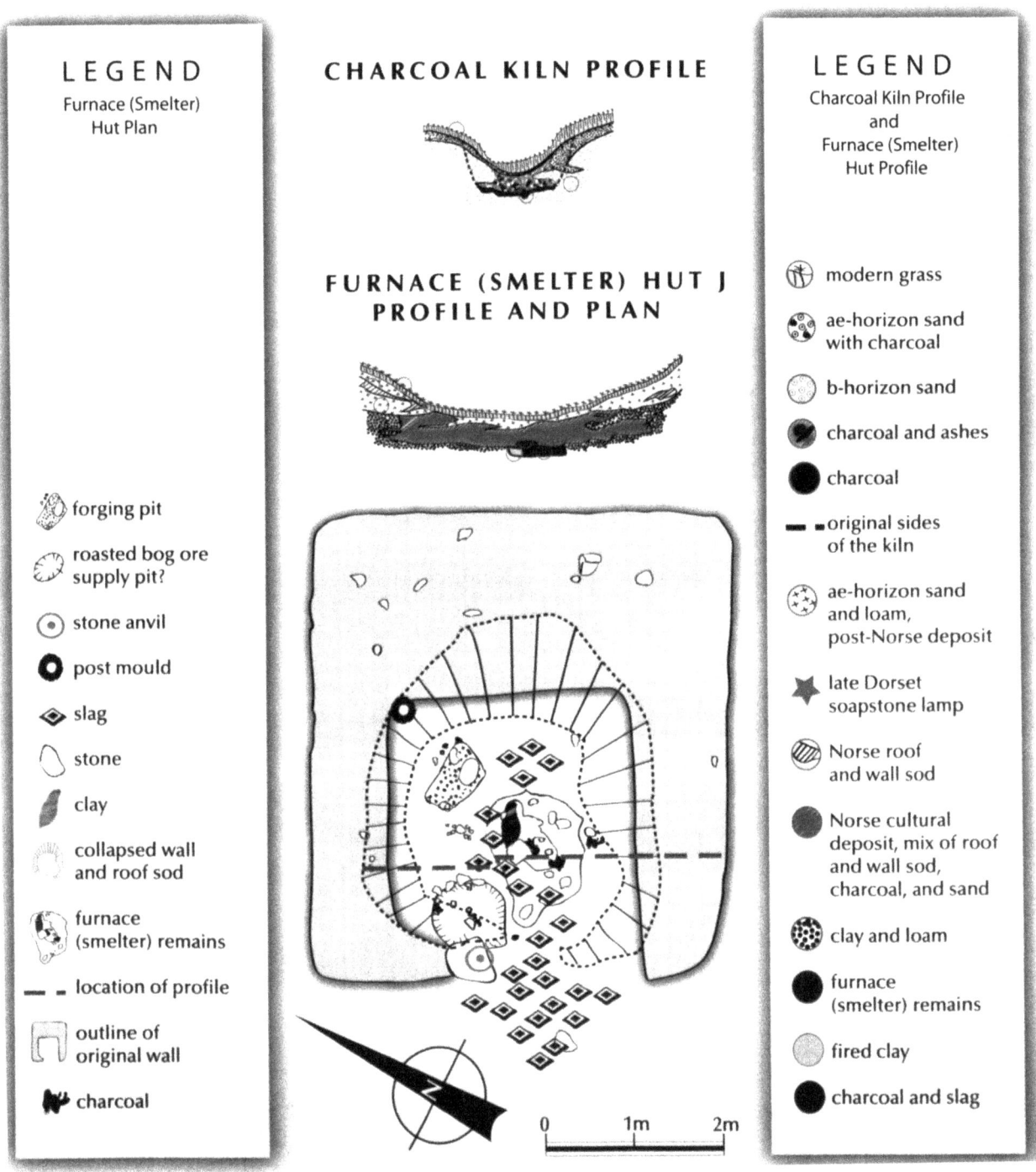

Fig. 2.31b, Wallace's plan of Smithy J (After Wallace 2006, 62)

Cooking Pit II was found shortly to the northeast of Hall F, measuring 3 m in diameter and 70 cm deep (Fig. 2.34a and 2.34b) (Petré 1985, 66). Its use as a cooking pit can be inferred from the heating of the stones and the stratigraphy of the fill, which indicates that at least two large fires had been lit within the pit (Petré 1985, 68). The pit was lined with a compact layer of charcoal, 5 cm deep in the center and increasing to a 20 cm depth along the side. This layer contained both charcoal dust and pieces of wood charcoal up to 10 cm in diameter. Above the charcoal lay "brittle-burned stones of varying sizes" along the edges of the pit, leaving the center filled with soot. Petré interpreted this as another cooking pit, which in such proximity to Hall F could most likely be attributed to the Norse (1985, 68); radiocarbon dating later confirmed that both cooking pits were dug during

the period of Norse occupation, and the presence of slag within close proximity to the hearths suggested that the cooking pits were contemporary with the Norse occupation (A.S. Ingstad 1985c, 241–5). Ingstad thus concluded that the two cooking pits from "the earliest days of Norse settlement, were used while the people were still busy building their turf houses" (A.S. Ingstad 1985c, 242).

Fig. 2.33b, Photo of Cooking Pit I (After Eldjárn 1985, 105)

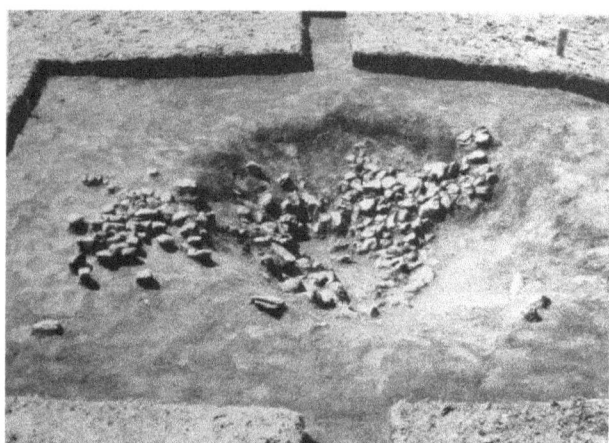

Fig. 2.34a, Photo of Cooking Pit II (After A.S. Ingstad 1985b, 74)

Fig. 2.33a, Plan of Cooking Pit I (After A.S. Ingstad 1985, Pl. 43)

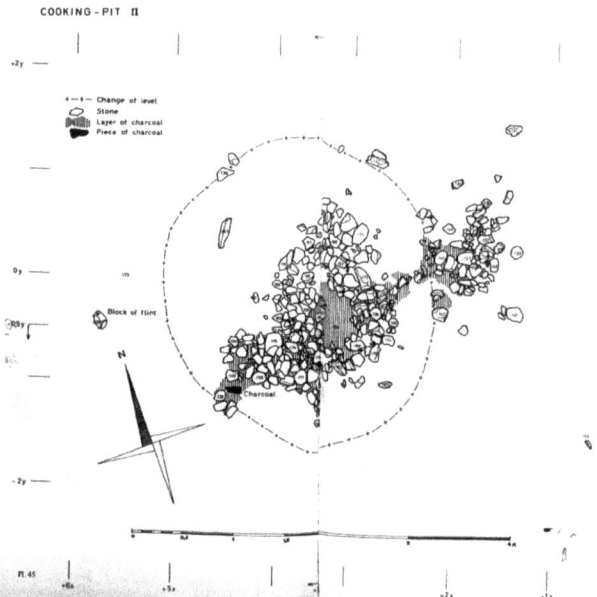

Fig. 2.34b, Plan of Cooking Pit II (After A.S. Ingstad 1985, Pl. 45)

Boat Sheds: Archaeological Description and Analysis

The presence of boats at the site can be assumed from the fact that the Norse somehow had to reach North America from Greenland. The excavation of boat sheds on the beach, however, provided concrete evidence of where boats could have been stored at the site. Though the sheds would not have been large enough to contain large, open-ocean vessels, they would have been sufficient for smaller, coastal crafts.

The Ingstads concluded that the depressions between the Smithy and Épaves Bay on the western shore of Black Duck Brook were, in fact, boat sheds: "The profiles clearly revealed that the depressions were the work of man, that they had been dug into the bank, and that the loose soil had been heaped up on the sides, after which stacked turfs to form the walls were added" (Christensen 1985, 123). Excavations by Wallace and Parks Canada confirmed the presence of four or five boatsheds laid in a row, a "typical west Nordic custom" (Ingstad 1971, 191). The sheds contained no small finds of any significance, though upon its floor lay two pieces of whalebone, which may have lain in the sand before the construction of the sheds, or could have been brought in by the boats (Christensen 1985, 123–5).

The construction of the boat sheds was difficult to determine, as the shoreline has undergone active erosion over the last millennium. Enough of the original structure remained, however, that Ingstad's team deduced that the walls had been constructed from gravel and stacked turfs, after a shallow depression had been dug into the soil of the bank (Christensen 1985, 125). There was no evidence that posts had been used to support a roof, and it was concluded that the turf walls may have been thick enough to support the roof on their own (Christensen 1985, 127–9). Recent excavation analyses have suggested that there were posts, but that they were placed closer to the walls, to allow for a more open space in between in which to place the boats. When compared to contemporary boat sheds in Scandinavia the sheds at L'Anse aux Meadows appeared "unusually short and wide" (Christensen 1985, 129). Norwegian coastal settlements, however, had boat sheds which housed smaller boats that would have been used along the coast (Christensen 1985, 132), rather than in open water. These *naust* were used for storing smaller boats, as well as for storing fishing gear, and were typically placed "as close to the shore as possible, preferably with a gently sloping beach in front, in order to facilitate the work of launching and landing the boats as much as possible" (Christensen 1985, 132).

Naust are still in use in Norway (Christensen 1985, 132), and it appeared that the boat sheds at L'Anse aux Meadows were indeed of this type. Each *naust* on the shore of Épaves Bay held one boat, which Ingstad believed to indicate that "every one of which belonged to one of the houses on the terrace;" thus, the presence of so many *naust* on the shore suggests that all three complexes on the terraces were most likely occupied at the same time (A.S. Ingstad 1985d, 267). There is sufficient archaeological evidence to prove that the Norse were indeed exploring the North American coast, as particular materials excavated at L'Anse aux Meadows can only be found in more southern regions. Some pieces of the worked wood found in the bog came from the butternut (*Juglans cinerea*) tree, as did three the butternuts found with them. This New World species can be found only as far north at the St. Lawrence Valley and the Miramichi River in New Brunswick; their presence on the site is "best explained as the result of transportation to the site by humans" (Wallace 1990, 193). Such evidence proves that someone at L'Anse aux Meadows visited the land further south. The association with the Norse cultural complex comes from its presence within the worked wood at the terrace edge of the peat bog, amongst other artifacts which are undoubtedly Norse.

Analysis of Building Construction

As noted above, buildings at L'Anse aux Meadows lacked stone foundations, but were built as solidly as local materials allowed. Wallace has shown that each building was constructed in one incident, with all of the smaller rooms within Halls A, D, and F being built during the initial phase of construction, rather than added on at a later time, as Ingstad proposed; sods in the corner walls connecting the rooms were placed in an interlocking pattern, which suggests that all rooms were contemporaneous There were no repairs or alterations evident in the patterns of turf (Wallace 1990, 183). Each wall consisted of an inner core of sand, gravel, and earth, enclosed by the strips of turf (Wallace 1990, 175). The fact that many of the interior walls as well were constructed out of turf rather than wood indicated that each room could support its own roof, without reliance on a supply of wood (Wallace 1990, 178).

The Halls, as well as House B, "were constructed of sod over a timber frame" (Wallace 1990, 174). After the sod walls had been constructed, the wooden frame was placed within the walls, and the roof built over it; analysis of the wooden timbers in several of the halls revealed that "they were made of local wood such as Balsam fir" (Wallace 2006, 51). Halls A and F contained two rows of posts in the interior of most of their rooms, along with occasional posts along the side walls of other rooms (Wallace 1990, 174). All of the smaller structures, except for Hut C, also had post holes inside, which indicated that posts were used to hold up their roofs; Hut C lacked evidence of posts, but the excess of sod inside the walls suggests that the roof was most likely built in an Icelandic false-cupola technique (Wallace 1990, 174), in which the blocks and strips of sod used to make the walls would begin to be piled inward, using the pressure of their weight against the other walls to create and maintain a sod roof. Thus, a wooden post structure would not have been needed to support a roof.

Comparison of construction techniques of the buildings at L'Anse aux Meadows to those of buildings at contemporary Scandinavian sites not only confirmed that the site on Épaves Bay was Norse, but also suggested elements of construction of which no trace remains. While Greenland houses generally lack evidence of internal wooden support for the roof, Icelandic houses frequently had roofs supported by wooden posts (A.S. Ingstad 1985c, 181). The rows of post holes—double or single—excavated at L'Anse aux Meadows fit with the construction patterns of Norse dwellings of the saga period. No evidence of traditional Norse windows (*gluggr*), smoke-holes (*ljóri*), or doors (*hurð*) remained. The construction of these turf buildings and comparisons to similar sites in the Norse cultural sphere, however, allow for the educated presumption that such doors and windows would have also been present in the buildings at L'Anse aux Meadows, even if adaptations to this frontier context required that the traditional form be altered.

In an effort to better understand the Norse construction techniques employed, Parks Canada built replicas of the buildings at the Historic Site at L'Anse aux Meadows (Fig. 2.35). After constructing the replicas, Parks Canada calculated that such a settlement would require either sixty men to construct the entire Norse settlement in two months, or ninety men in a month and a half, not including the time needed to cut the sod (Wallace 2000b, 380). With the amount of time and labor invested, it is surprising that the sod walls were not constructed with stone foundations, in order to be more permanent.

The location of the buildings in relation to one another suggested a contemporaneous settlement. Hall A, as an Icelandic *skáli* with few of the Greenland modifications in room positioning, represented "the earliest type of dwelling house on the terrace;" as it appeared to be contemporary with Houses B and C; Ingstad thus believed it likely that this complex was the first built on the terrace above Épaves Bay, particularly considering the important supply of fresh water nearby in Black Duck Brook (A.S. Ingstad 1985c, 233). Wallace, however, believed Complex A-B-C to have been built last on the site, as its placement in relation to Black Duck Brook and its flooding suggests poor planning (Wallace 2000a, 177). Indeed, this supports the conclusion that Hall F had been the residence of the leader of the expedition. If all three buildings were constructed at the same time, and Hall F was the largest of the halls, a logical conclusion would be that the leader on the site would live there.

An argument for contemporaneous construction amongst all three Complexes may also be made by the artifact distribution, which appeared to assign one particular function necessary for site operation to each group of buildings (Wallace 1990, 182); this specialization between complexes was mirrored by the differences in building layout amongst them, which may indicate differences in social structure among the groups occupying each one (Wallace 1990, 183).

Conclusion of Site Layout and Excavations

All three building complexes on the terrace above Épaves Bay, as well as outlying structures such as the Smithy and boat sheds, have been conclusively identified as Norse. The archaeological remains at L'Anse aux Meadows will be further analyzed in subsequent chapters. Certain noted attributes and features will be considered in light of the site as a whole: the lack of stone foundations, the particular use of fire features, the artifact evidence, and the construction of certain buildings.

Complex D-E: Archaeological Analysis

Fig. 2.35, Photo of the reconstruction of Complex A-B-C at the National Parks Site at L'Anse aux Meadows. (Author)

CHAPTER 3 Artifact Evidence and Analyses

The results of the archaeological investigations of the structures at L'Anse aux Meadows have been presented, and it is clear that they belong to the Norse cultural complex. We will now turn to the artifact evidence and analyses to determine how the site functioned.

Preservation conditions "were as poor as they could be" on the acidic terrace (Ingstad 1971, 192). Most of the artifacts were excavated by Parks Canada in the peat bog, and while most were made of iron, many were made of organic materials, particularly wood (Wallace 1977, "Norse," 5); they were found in the greatest numbers within 6 m of the edge of the terrace (Schonback et. al. 1976, 17).

Wallace has divided the artifacts into six categories:

1) small, personal "lost" articles;
2) a few domestic objects sufficiently simple and easily replaceable to be left behind when the site was abandoned;
3) carpentry debitage;
4) broken and discarded wooden objects;
5) boatnails;
6) iron slag from both smelting and smithing. (Wallace 1990: 176)

As relatively few artifacts were found at L'Anse aux Meadows, those which can give deeper insight into the activities and purpose of the site deserve a brief discussion.

Norse Diagnostic Artifacts

Several artifacts which allowed the identification of the site as Norse were found: iron fragments and a whole nail (Fig 3.1), pieces of jasper, a piece of copper (Hall D, Room III) (Fig. 3.2), a bronze ring-headed pin (Fig. 2.8), and a bone needle (from Hall D) (Fig. 3.3), a stone lamp, and a needle hone (Ingstad 1971, 192).

In the Norse occupational layer above the hearth in Room III of Hall D was a small, damaged copper alloy object; this piece of copper may have been used in a belt, as it was covered with cross-stripings. Metallurgical analyses show that it also contained other minerals besides copper, and, thus, that it had been smelted. Such techniques preclude the possibility of the object belonging to an indigenous culture, as the copper native to the area is almost pure, and is worked by hammering, not smelting (Ingstad 1971, 183). The ring-headed pin, found on the edge of the cooking pit in Room III of Hall A, is of a Norse type dated to the ninth and tenth centuries, and betrays Irish influences in its design (A.S. Ingstad 1985d, 256).

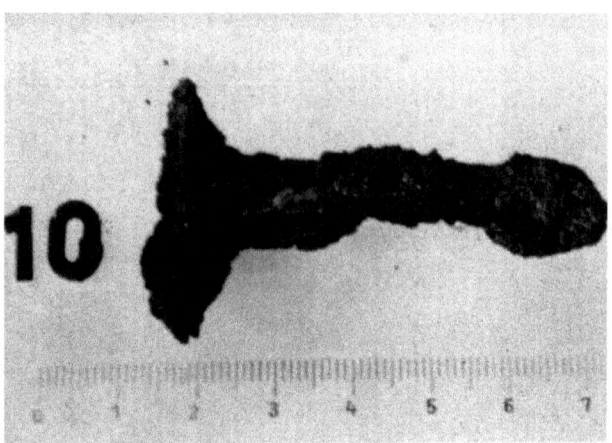

LaM 60 (Sample No. 10).
Fig. 3.1, The only whole nail found on the site (After Rosenqvist 1985, Fig. 1)

Fig. 3.2, Copper fragment from Hall D, Room III (After Petré 1985, 62)

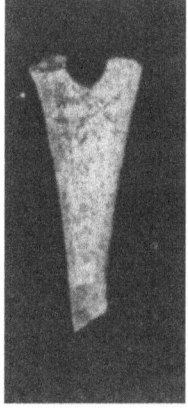

Fig. 3.3, Bone needle from Hall D (After Petré 1985, 63)

Artifact Evidence and the Origins of the Inhabitants of L'Anse aux Meadows

Ten strike-a-lights (Fig. 3.4) made of red jasper were found in total on the site, two in Complex A-B-C, two in Complex D-E, and five in Complex F-G, while a last piece was found on the terrace (Wallace 2006, 82). These pieces of jasper were analyzed and sourced using Instrumental Neutron Activation Analysis by comparing their signature to those of known jasper sources in Iceland, Greenland, and Newfoundland (Smith 2000,

217). Four of the five pieces from F-G were from western Greenland, while one was from western Iceland; those of A-B-C and D-E were all from Iceland (Wallace 2006, 82). As these artifacts are "always personal objects," Wallace concluded that the occupants of Hall F were from Greenland, whereas the inhabitants of A-B-C and D-E were from Iceland (Wallace 2006, 82).

Fig. 3.4, Jasper strike-a-lights from L'Anse aux Meadows; Left to right, 1 piece (Norse occupation) from Newfoundland, 1 piece (Native American occupation) from Newfoundland, 4 pieces from Greenland, and 5 pieces from Iceland (After Wallace 2006, 83)

Analysis of the building layouts at L'Anse aux Meadows may be able to suggest the origins of their inhabitants. Hall A resembled the Icelandic *skáli* and very early phases of settlement in Greenland and the North Atlantic, such as the houses at Narssaq and Jarlshof. Hall D has already been discussed as a *Þorsárdalur-type* hall, a layout particular to Iceland. It could also be interpreted as an early passage house, as Room II is slightly offset from the larger hall, yet was used as living space; in this case, the house could be considered of Greenland origin, though of a very early variety. Hall D resembles several longhouses from the early phases of settlement in Greenland: Hvalsey, the Farm Beneath the Sand, Narssaq, and Brattahlid, albeit a smaller version of such. Halls A and D based upon building layout thus could be either of Icelandic or early Greenlandic origins, due to the similarities between the two. Such a combination suggests that the settlers in Halls A and D were from Greenland or aware of Greenland adaptations, while others were from Iceland. Hall F, in contrast, was a clear example of the Greenland passage house adaptation of the Norse *skáli*, which thus indicates that its inhabitants were from Greenland.

Combining artifact and building evidence, Wallace concluded that three separate groups of people came in boats to Newfoundland at the same time, and that based upon artifact and construction evidence, the inhabitants of Complexes A-B-C and D-E retained Icelandic cultural traditions, while those of Complex F-G used the newer Greenland adaptations (Wallace 2000c, 212–3). This combination of inhabitants from Greenland and Iceland fits the Vinland settlement model.

Artifact Dating

Several objects found outside of Complex D-E can provide a date for the occupation of the site. A small bone used to bore holes, found near Hut E, "has a parallel in Jorvik [Viking Age York, England] which would make it no later than the 10th century" (Wallace 1990, 180). A small wooden arrow, made of white cedar, which did not grow near the site during the Norse occupation, "resembles the 11th century arrowheads of antler found at Umiviarssuk and Narssaq in Greenland and has the same proportions" (Wallace 1990, 180). The discarded objects included a plank of spruce, which had been attached as a patch to a broken boat strake with two wooden nails; similar patches were used in Viking Dublin (10th–11th centuries) to repair boats (Wallace 1990, 180). These artifacts appear similar to those from the 10th and 11th centuries, suggesting a date for occupation.

Domestic Artifacts

The spindle whorl, 3.5 cm in diameter, was "curved and sooty underneath and was probably made from the fragment of a lamp or a pot" (Fig. 3.5a) (Ingstad 1971, 185); it had been crafted after the soapstone had been blackened, as the soot is present on the whorl's concave bottom, but not on the carved sides (A.S. Ingstad 1985c, 223). This spindle whorl is similar in construction to those belonging to the early phase of occupation at Jarlshof, which were made of various materials such as soapstone, sandstone, bone, and pottery sherds, and all measured between 3 and 5 cm in diameter (Fig. 3.6) (Hamilton 1956).

Helge Ingstad believed the presence of the spindle whorl to indicate that "there must have been women at L'Anse aux Meadows" (Ingstad 1971, 185). The wool, Ingstad supposed, "must probably have come from their own sheep" (Ingstad 1971, 185). However, there was no conclusive evidence of livestock of any kind being kept or raised on the site, so the wool spun on the spindle whorl was probably brought to the site. Wallace reasoned that the transport of wool to the site could have happened without the transport of sheep, as "it is possible that the settlers carried bags of unspun wool to occupy themselves over the winter months or on days with bad weather" (Wallace 2006, 68). The fragment of bone needle from Hall D and the needle hone from Hall F provided conclusive evidence that some sort of sewing or needlework was done at L'Anse aux Meadows.

Fig. 3.5, The spindle whorl from L'Anse aux Meadows (After A.S. Ingstad 1985, Fig. 48)

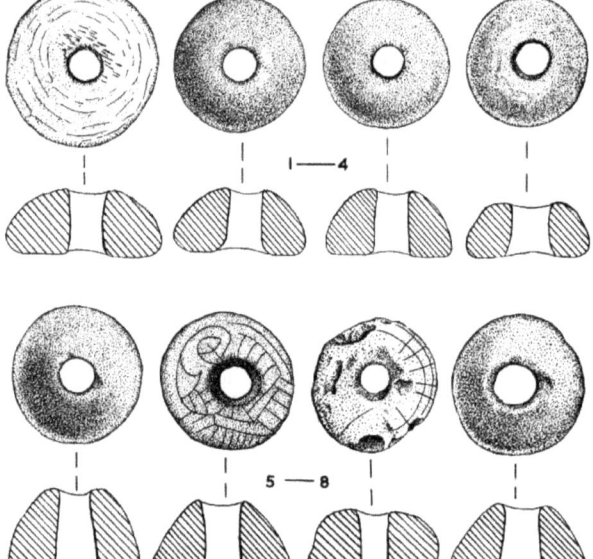

Fig. 3.6 Several examples of spindle whorls found at Jarlshof (After Hamilton 1956, 144)

A group of domestic artifacts was also found in Hut E: a heap of nineteen fist-sized pieces of limestone, which have been interpreted as possible loom weights or fishing weights. There is no published photograph of these stones. There is no doubt that these stones found in Hut E were used as weights—both Ingstad and Wallace agreed on this point. Ingstad concluded that they were used as fishing weights, while Wallace concluded that they may have been used as loom weights (Wallace 2006, 68). The stones could have been used for either purpose.

Loom and fishing weights were both excavated at Jarlshof. All were made of soapstone or other materials, and were divided into two groups based on size and shape. The first was ovaloid, with an incised hole at the top, and measuring roughly 12 cm by 8 cm and weighing between ½ and 1 pound; the second group was described as "water-worn pebbles of schistose rock generally oval in form with flat surfaces" (Fig. 3.7) (Hamilton 1956, 117) (117 IMG Jarlshof). Excavations also uncovered 11 line-sinkers, all of which were grooved in some manner to facilitate the attachment of line for use in fishing (Figs. 3.7 and 3.8) (Hamilton 1956).

In light of other archaeological evidence in Hut E, however, to be discussed in Chapter 5, the nineteen fist-sized stones were most likely used as loom weights.

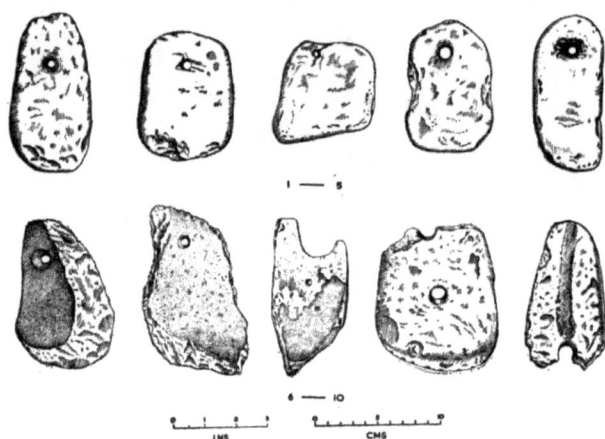

Fig. 3.7, Weights from Jarlshof, (1–8, soapstone loom weights, 9–10 soapstone fishing weights) (After Hamilton 1956, 117)

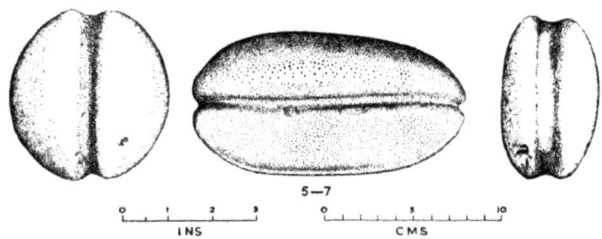

Fig. 3.8, Sandstone fishing weights from Jarlshof (After Hamilton 1956, 118)

Carpentry Debris and Wooden Artifacts

The presence of large forests in Newfoundland, so different from the scanty woodlands of Iceland and Greenland, must have been a fortuitous discovery for the Norse at L'Anse aux Meadows. Wooden objects were recovered with the most ease among all the artifacts of the site, as the peat bog behind the terrace provided excellent preservation conditions for organic materials. One of the objects in the bog was small sewn birch-bark container filled with stone that "might have been a netsinker of a kind that has been found on late Viking Period and early Medieval sites in Sweden" (Fig. 3.9). Such a weight would have allowed for greater ease in catching the abundant quantities of cod off the coast of Newfoundland, which animal bone evidence at the site indicate were consumed during the Norse occupation.

Fig. 3.9, Small birchbark container found in the bog. (After S. Vandervloogt. in Wallace 2000a, 174)

Of the wood on the terrace, the majority "was encountered in the bog margin immediately outside and a short distance [15 m] north and south of the D-E complex" (Wallace 1990, 184), while a comparatively meager amount was found outside Complexes A-B-C and F-G. As preservation conditions are equivalent along the entire bog margin, Wallace determined that "the carpentry must have been limited to the D-E area" (Wallace 1990, 184). In confirmation of Wallace's inference that the wood-working had taken place at Complex D-E, a number of wooden objects were found within that complex: "a broken bow for a carpenter's auger and a floorboard for a small boat...several treenails and pieces of rope made from fine spruce roots (Fig. 3.10) [and] stumps of planks that had been cut radially from a log" (Wallace 2006, 64). Evidence of repeated carpentry activities, however, was difficult to obtain, as the deposit showed no discernible stratification—the deposit could be from one episode of wood-working or from successive episodes within a short period of time (Wallace 1990, 182).

Wallace's excavations uncovered the majority of the wood debris. Carpentry scraps and cut wood were found in two general areas: some lay among the driftwood, but most was along the boundary between the terrace and the bog (Wallace, "1976 Excavations," 1977, 5). The majority of the wood was larch (*Larix laricina*) or balsam fir (*Abies balsamea*), while tiny fragments of pine (*Pinus resinsoa* or *Pinus sylvestris*), which is not native to Newfoundland, indicate a European connection for the inhabitants at L'Anse aux Meadows (Wallace 1990, 184). Of the 1,467 pieces of wood found along the bog during the 1973–1976 Parks Canada excavations, 644 were deposited during the Norse occupation (Wallace 2006, 66), and "their distribution in the bog would indicate the level of the contemporary bog surface" (Wallace, "1976 Excavations," 1977, 5). The carpentry debitage from the Norse period consisted of roughly a thousand small pieces, mostly from chipping, axing, and whittling (Wallace 1990, 182–4). Analysis of the wood debitage by Paul Gleeson further determined that the wood attributed stratigraphically to the Norse occupation had been cut with a metal tool: of these scraps, 64% were "waste from felling and cutting with an axe or adze," while other chips had been whittled (Wallace 2006, 67).

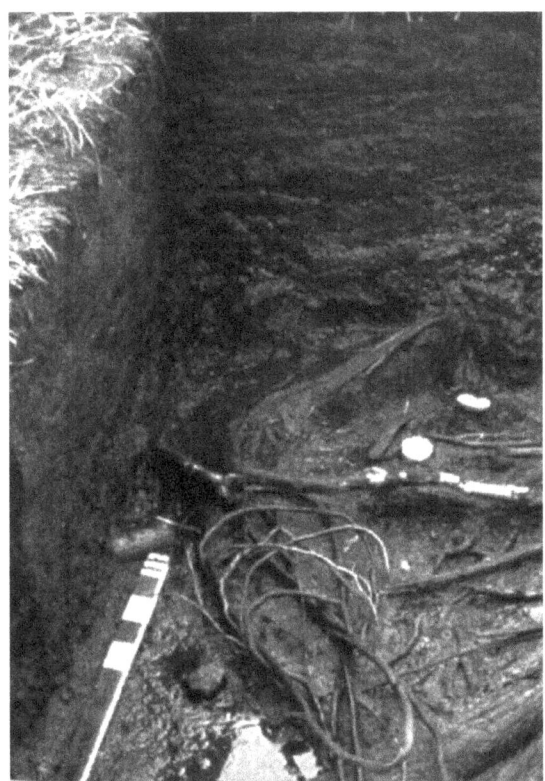

Fig. 3.10, Coiled spruce roots (After D. Brown. in Wallace 2000a, p 172)

Iron Smelting and Smithing

Iron production at L'Anse aux Meadows has already been discussed briefly in the interpretation of the use of the Smithy. Iron was smelted from the bog ore found in the peat bog behind the terrace, where dissolved hematite in the water accumulated on marsh grass; Norse iron working commonly involved the gathering of such ore (Jóhannesson 2006, 300–1). The process of extracting such iron was "well-known in the Norse region." To the Norse, whose weapons and tools were largely made of iron, Ingstad wrote that the site "must have been a virtual eldorado," as a large amount of ore could be easily extracted from the peat bog (Ingstad and Ingstad 2000, 153). In Greenland, iron was worked with simple tools, and in turn was used to make a variety of incredibly useful tools: knives, axes, sickles, scythes, forging tongs, sheep-shears, sledge-hammers, awls, chisels, arrowheads, spears, tweezers, horseshoes, boat rivets, etc. (Ingstad and Ingstad 2000, 16–7).

Most important for analysis of site activity are those artifacts associated with the smelting of bog ore into usable iron, which was then worked on the site. Activities involving iron included its smelting and forging, and then its subsequent use in boat repair or construction. Thus, the act of smelting itself, which was not done by the native populations in Newfoundland, indicated that the site at L'Anse aux Meadows is of Norse origin.

The use of a separate outbuilding, like Smithy J, to work iron was a common practice on Norse farms (Ingstad and Ingstad 2000, 16). Evidence for the production of iron from local bog ore has been shown at several Icelandic sites (Vésteinsson 2000, 169), specifically that at the farmstead at Háls (c. 1000–1275 CE) in western Iceland (Smith 2005, 187–9). This Icelandic site contained substantial evidence of iron production, including a slag heap covering 45 m^2, several smaller accumulated piles of slag, and "a cluster of production features including furnace bases, pits, and smithy debris forming an arc around the western end of the main slag heap" (Smith 2005, 188). Several episodes of iron periods of iron production, each including many individual episodes of smelting, occurred every 30 to 60 years. The main slag heap contained more than 5000 kg or slag, the biproduct of 22,300 kg of charcoal and 6200 kg of bog ore, used to produce 1400 kg of workable iron (Smith 2005, 195–6). Smith calculated that such an amount "would have taken nearly 140 smelts…with a team of three to five metalworkers putting in more than 9200 person-days of labor from start to finish" (Smith 2005, 196). The usable iron production of L'Anse aux Meadows (3 kg), in comparison, would equal 2.15% of the usable iron at Háls. Other Icelandic sites with small-scale (less than 150 kg of slag) iron-working include Grelutóttir, Herjólfsdalur, and Reykjavík (Smith 1995, 335).

In smelting, the bog ore would have first been roasted, its water burnt off over fresh wood. The dried bog ore would have then been packed into the furnace with great quantities of charcoal. This charcoal, which would have been produced nearby, was necessary for the removal of iron from bog ore, as it burns at a higher temperature than fresh wood and allows for the hotter fire needed for smelting. As the bog ore burned, the slag would separate from the iron, which would drip to the bottom and form a sponge. After the first firing had been finished, the iron sponge, known as a bloom, would be hammered into a billet at an even higher temperature to remove more impurities before the iron would have been ready to forge (Wallace 2000c, 212).

This was the process which occurred at L'Anse aux Meadows. Comparison between the bog ores sampled from inside the Smithy and elsewhere on the site showed that both had the same chemical components (iron oxides, lepidocorcite, and goethite), and thus that the bog ore used in smelting in building J was taken from the site at L'Anse aux Meadows (Rosenqvist 1985, 421). Once the bog ore had first been roasted, the furnace was smashed and the slag raked down the bank (Wallace 2000c, 212). Of the total 15 kg of slag excavated, "practically all" of it lay within or immediately surrounding the Smithy (Wallace 1990, 185), and eighty-six percent of the total slag excavated came from smelting and its associated products (Wallace 2000a, 173). These 15 kg are the result of a "small, one-time firing," and resulted in only 3 kg or usable iron, demonstrating that "the skills of the iron workers had not been great" (Wallace 2000a, 173). Though the total weight of collected iron was 10 kg, and no more than 7 kg of it was smithable, "it was assumed that another 5 kg remained uncollected in and around the furnace hut" (Wallace 2006, 62).

Chemical analysis of the slag shows that the oven in the Smithy at L'Anse aux Meadows had reached a temperature of 2,282°F (1,250°C) when smelting (Wallace 2000c, 212), and that the iron "had been made by the direct-reduction process, the type of process used at…other Viking-Age iron manufacture sites…so called because the iron produced could be forged directly into iron implements before any other type of refinement took place" (Wallace 2006, 62). This type of refinement made the immediate crafting of tools possible, but not necessary. An "exhaustive" metallurgical study by John Stewart and Henry Unglik of Parks Canada's Conservation Division showed the various types of slag to have been manufactured, in fact, as the end result of three separate refining processes (Wallace 2006, 62).

The Parks Canada team searched in their 1976 excavations for evidence of another smelting pit, since the small quantity of smelting slag was puzzling. Iron smelting in Norway and Sweden was recognizable from the presence of large heaps of slag, but there were no such heaps at L'Anse aux Meadows; the only slag found at the site was inside the Smithy (Wallace, "1976 Excavations," 1977, 6). Wallace believed that the fire pit in the northern end of the Smithy "may have been for forging, as the only finds directly associated with it were five small lumps of slag, and a few pieces of forging slag" (Wallace 1990, 185). The iron-slag ratio at Norse sites was typically 1:3; using this calculation, only "a little over 3 kg of iron was worked at L'Anse aux

Meadows," which indicated that such activity had been on a household scale (Wallace, "1976 Excavations," 1977, 6). This paucity of iron working on the site coincides with the relatively small number of nails produced. Ultimately, however, if only a few nails were needed for repair, there would be no need for extensive iron production, which would explain why the Parks Canada team failed to find evidence of such.

The majority of the iron found at L'Anse aux Meadows was scrap, slag or rust—only a few, rare identifiable objects were found, in a pattern similar to the rest of the Norse North Atlantic (Vésteinsson 2000, 169). The only *whole* nail was in the bog outside of Hall D (Wallace 2006, 63); with this exception, the identifiable objects are *all* discarded boat nails (Wallace 1990, 186). Eighty to a hundred iron pieces have been retrieved and interpreted as nail fragments; though the quantity seems relatively small by modern standards, the Norse normally used iron nails for boat repair, and used them only infrequently for house construction (Wallace 1990, 184; Wallace 2006, 63). Furthermore, 66% of the nail fragments on the site were found in Complex F-G, particularly in Room VI on the eastern side of Hall F; the rest were scattered over the site (Wallace 2006, 64). "The nail shanks were clipped and the roves deliberately cut from the edge to the centre so that they could be pried loose;" similar mutilated nails were used to repair boats at the Paviken trade port in Sweden (Wallace 1990, 185). The discarded nails in Hall F have a different chemical composition from the iron produced in the Smithy; thus, Hall F can be interpreted as a center for boat repair at L'Anse aux Meadows, where the original nails used to build the ship in the North Atlantic were replaced with brand-new forged nails from L'Anse aux Meadows (Wallace 1990, 184–5).

The locations of the different products of ironworking throughout the site may indicate which particular activities were designated to each complex and their inhabitants. The majority (7% of total) of the smithing-hearth slag was found in the Smithy, with the exception of two lumps, one in House B and one in Hall F (Wallace 2006, 62). Wallace proposed that bog ore had been roasted in House B, where the cultural layer contained a wide and deep deposit of fine ash mixed with small pieces of bog ore, roasted between layers of firewood which smoldered for several hours (Wallace 2006, 60). Five percent of the total slag came from blacksmith work, mostly in Complex A-B-C (Wallace 2006, 62); Wallace determined that since this slag "is chiefly in the southernmost hall [A]," the actual forging had taken place in Hall A (Wallace 2000a, 176).

Wallace believed that iron production "was not been planned but arose when one of the boats had been damaged. The various duties were then divided among the three households, perhaps on the basis of expertise" (Wallace 2000a, 177). As smelting was not practiced on every Norse farm, since the quantity and presence of bog ore varied among homesteads (Jóhannesson 2006, 301), it is likely that some of the men at L'Anse aux Meadows had greater familiarity with smelting than did others, and that a professional smith had been specifically included on the voyage (Wallace 1990, 187). Large quantities of smithing slag and several iron nails have been found within the hearth and midden of Room III, Hall A; smaller quantities of slag and bog ore were also present in the ember pit of House B. It would thus appear that small amounts of bog ore were smelted within Complex A-B-C, perhaps indicating that the master smith of the settlement lived in this complex.

Boat Repair

The majority of activity debris at L'Anse aux Meadows—iron slag, carpentry scraps, nail bits—stems from the repair of boats, which suggests that the main activity at the site was boat repair. Wallace emphasized that "boats and ships were nearly the only places where the West Norse used iron nails" (2006, 64); thus, their presence in such relative abundance among the debitage of carpentry work and planks of wood in Complex D-E suggests ship repair.

The whole nail found in the bog west of Hall D was hand-forged, with a large square head and a square cross-section, measuring 9 cm long (Wallace, "1976 Excavations," 1977, 3). This nail was the only one found on the site made from the iron in the local bog ore, and was probably dropped during construction and repair (Wallace 2000c, 212). Thus, all of the other locally-produced nails sailed away with the Norse when the settlement was abandoned. Five meters to the south of this nail was the bundle of two coiled roots, which could have been used used for tying and lashing of wooden planks for the construction of boats; such techniques are common in the Norse cultural sphere, as "the upper strakes of Viking vessels were lashed together, not nailed or riveted," and thus "it is tempting to associate the bundle of roots with boat repair" (Wallace, "1976 Excavations," 1977, 4). The quantity of nails found, however, indicated that the ship repair done on site was not of great magnitude. In the Gokstad ship, the 3,500 nails holding the ship together each had an average weight of 28 g and a total combined weight of roughly 100kg. The 80–100 nails at L'Anse aux Meadows paled in comparison, and suggested that the ship repair was not on a large scale (Wallace 1990, 186). Similarly, commercial iron manufacture at Møsstrund in Norway produced 1000 kg (Wallace 2006, 62). This contrast in quantity suggested that the ship repair was not intentionally planned, but arose from necessity.

Boat repair at the site is suggested not only by the iron smelting and smithing at the site, but also by the wooden evidence in Complex D-E: the wooden stumps of planks were "invariably...used as boat planks" (Wallace 2006, 64); indeed, Wallace concluded that "the purpose of much of the carpentry seems to have been repair," with an assemblage similar to that on the island of Falster in Denmark, which was also a boat repair site (Wallace 1990, 184). The work of replacing old planks with new ones "left its mark in the form of nail fragments scattered over the floor and the ground around it". Wallace argued that the occasional presence of iron nails within fire features, such as in Room II of Hall F, was a result of the use of discarded or damaged boat planks as fuel (Wallace 2006, 46). It is also possible that the inhabitants of L'Anse aux Meadows used the discarded planks of wood from boat repair within Hall F as seating upon the benches which appear to have been present around several of the long hearths in the other buildings on the terrace.

As most of the iron nails and carpentry debris were found in Room VI of Hall F, it is likely that this room was used for boat repair. At many West Norse sites, "such quantities of iron nails are only found on sites where boats and ships have undergone repairs, which is undoubtedly what took place here" (Wallace 2000c, 211). This boat repair integrated the iron manufacture, the smithing, and the carpentry. Room VI of Hall F seemed to have been built for a specific purpose not originally intended or included in the initial building plans, as the walls of the room had been built directly over grass (Wallace 2006, 46), further suggesting that the creation of iron nails from bog ore and the resulting boat repair arose out of necessity, and were not originally planned.

Wallace concluded that it is "perhaps significant that the boat repair took place by Hall F. We have already concluded that this was probably the residence of the leader, and it is only natural that the leader wished to exert his control over this work" (Wallace 2006, 64). Here small boats known as *faerings* (Wallace 2000a, 177), which would have fit both in the boat sheds along the bay and in Room VI, were repaired. Iron smelting and forging at the site was done solely for the production of iron nails with which to repair the boats, and either in one incident or in several smaller incidents in quick succession. Such necessity for boat repair, and the presence of smaller boats, indicates that small, coastal explorations were underway from L'Anse aux Meadows.

Purpose and Central Activity of the Site

The few artifacts recovered at L'Anse aux Meadows allow interpretation of life at the site. Certain skilled inhabitants of this Norse settlement collected bog ore from the peat bog behind their houses, smelted it, and forged it into usable nails when necessity dictated; such a knowledge of metalwork indicates that at least one craftsman skilled in iron smelting and forging lived in the settlement, probably in Complex A-B-C. The use of these nails on the site indicated that boats were at one point being repaired, as the Norse did not use iron nails for any other purpose; the discovery of planks of wood and carpentry debris corroborated this conclusion. The boats were stored in the boat sheds mentioned in Chapter 2, and were repaired in Room VI of Hall F, where most of the artifact evidence for boat repair appeared. The small size of Room VI suggests that some of the boats were small and maneuverable, and were most likely some sort of small craft for further exploration, in comparison with the larger ships with in the Norse must have sailed to Newfoundland.

CHAPTER 4: Dietary and Agricultural Practices at L'Anse aux Meadows

This chapter emphasizes dietary evidence from the site, such as hearth structures and faunal remains, in conjunction with the palynological evidence on climate, to conclude that typical Norse agricultural practices did not occur here. Unfortunately and inexplicably, macrobotanical analyses were not undertaken at L'Anse aux Meadows. Palynological investigations conducted on and around the site revealed that there has been no significant change in vegetation since the time of Norse occupation, nor in the millennium proceeding Norse arrival. There was no large-scale agriculture, as would be indicated by an interruption of pollen evidence resulting from the slash-and-burn method common in contemporary North Atlantic sites, particularly during the *landnám* in Iceland.

The type of faunal evidence recovered at the site, as well as the lack of archaeological evidence as would typically be expected of an early Norse settlement site, such as animal parasites, feed crops, and specific outbuildings used for animal shelter, also suggests that livestock were not kept on the site and that its inhabitants relied upon marine sources for food. There is a danger in relying on negative evidence, particularly when preservation conditions at the site are so poor. As Norse farming sites in the North Atlantic typically present certain signs of agricultural activity, however, their absence at L'Anse aux Meadows is worth noting, particularly since L'Anse aux Meadows does not appear to be a traditional farming settlement.

Dietary Adaptations to the North Atlantic: Iceland

Dietary practices in the North Atlantic followed the general Scandinavian Norse pattern; practices in Iceland, in tandem with climatic conditions, influenced dietary adaptations in Greenland. A brief description of Icelandic practices is therefore necessary before the particular Greenland practices are discussed.

Icelandic dietary and agricultural practices developed "entirely upon the pool of options and experience they imported from Europe along with their domestic animals and plants" (Vésteinsson et. al. 2002, 3). Norse arrival in Iceland was accompanied by the transformation of forests into grasslands as a result of early settlement *Landnám, which was* rapid and widespread (Vésteinsson et. al. 2002, 7). The anthropogenic rise in grasslands coincided with a marked decrease in forest cover. Early settlers used their new fields for the grazing of their livestock and the growing of crops, and their introduction of such methods of crop agriculture and of domesticated livestock "has been documented archaeologically and palynologically" (Smith 1995, 333).

Icelandic faunal assemblages of domestic animals "show consistent broad similarities in species composition" in a reliance on cattle, caprines, pigs, and horses (Vésteinsson et. al. 2002, 8). Fish and wild birds make up a substantial portion of the Icelandic faunal assemblages from the 10th- and 11th-centuries (Perdikaris and McGovern 2007, 199). The Norse also brought with them new species of flora and fauna which were not indigenous to Iceland, and which were associated with livestock, such as beetles and parasites (Smith 1995, 333–4).

The early Icelandic farmstead at Svalbarð provides a strong example of typical early settlement agricultural and dietary practices (McGovern et. al. 2000, 159. Located along a river, the site had a well-accumulated midden which yielded numerous faunal and botanical samples with which the farm's practices were reconstructed. Early in the farm's history, birds comprise up to 25% of the faunal assemblage, while whales appear later in settlement time. Overall, the assemblage is dominated by four groups: "cattle, caprines (both sheep and goats), fish (mostly Gadids) and seals" (Amorosi 1992, 123). Small quantities of other animals are also present. Species which occur "in trace amounts" include horse (*Equus caballus*), dog (*Canis familaris*), goat (*Capra hircus*), and pig (*Sus scrofa*) (Amorosi 1992, 123). Remains of fish such as cod (*Gadus morhua*) are abundant, and shellfish are comparatively rare. Overall, the typical Icelandic faunal diet as evidenced by the Svalbarð assemblage relied upon livestock such as cattle and sheep, wild game such as reindeer, and marine resources such as seals, whales, and fish.

Archaeobotanical analysis of the Svalbarð midden also provided evidence for agricultural practices at the site. The dominance of fen and grassland taxa (*Poaceae* and *Cyperacae*) and peat are interpreted as evidence of traditional Icelandic *landnám* land-clearance techniques. Similar transitions occurred in Norway as a result of such human impact, as well as livestock grazing (Zutter 1992, 143). The absence of "any type of cereal grains" was a marked difference from other Icelandic sites; this was interpreted as being caused by a "lack of favourable climatic conditions for grain growing in Northeastern Iceland, botanical preservation biases and/or animal husbandry begin the primary agrarian practice for the Svalbarð farm" (Zutter 1992, 144).

Dietary Adaptations to the North Atlantic: Greenland

To the greatest extent possible, the Norse who colonized Greenland from Iceland tried to maintain their traditional farms, although they did not bring the particular assemblage of domestic animals present in contemporary Iceland (McGovern et. al. 2000, 156). One major similarity between animal husbandry practices in Iceland and Greenland is the reliance upon cattle (Vésteinsson et. al. 2002, 9). Dairy played a large role in Norse North Atlantic diet: "it has been said that there is good pasture in Greenland, and there are great and good farms. The people have much cattle and many sheep, and they make large quantities of butter and cheese. They live chiefly on this, and on meat, and they also eat the meat of reindeer, whales, seals and bears" (Ingstad and Ingstad 2000, 16). Milk of both sheep and cows was generally prepared into curds (*skyr*), buttermilk (*saup*), and butter (*smjór*), while the whey (*mysa*) was drunk (Shetelig and Falk 1978: 311).

Methods of agriculture were the first to be adapted in Greenland. Grain was very difficult to grow in there, so difficult that most Greenlanders never saw bread (Ingstad and Ingstad 2000, 15–6). The only grain cultivated in Greenland was barley (Jóhannesson 2006, 297). Haymaking, to provide livestock with fodder, took a considerable amount of time and labor, as it had to be carried from meadows distant from farms, because nearer infields would be inhabited by grazing animals (Gad 1970, 39). The supply of hay for livestock commonly ran low, and it is not surprising that the settlers would seek other forms of sustenance than cultivated crops and domestic animals; the average farm had room for about only five cattle (Ingstad and Ingstad 2000, 16). As reported to the Pope during the early sixteenth century, the people in the diocese of Gardar in Greenland "because of the scarcity of bread, wine, and oil, live for the most part on dried fish and milk products" (quoted in Olson 1906, 73).

Initially, the Greenlanders expanded their diet to include wild game and marine foodstuffs; they "were essentially farmers who relied upon obtaining sufficient hay to overwinter their daily animals and balanced their diet with seal, bird, and caribou meat" (Buckland 2000, 148). The diet generally consisted of game meat, and substantial quantities of such remains have been found in Greenland middens: reindeer, polar hares, seals, walrus, the larger whale species (the right whale in particular, a subset of baleen wales which is now rare in the waters around Greenland), a few bears, Arctic foxes, and birds, as well as the *Gadus callarias* cod, which in modern times can be caught along the coast of Greenland. These same Greenland middens contained "few remains of domestic animals," while the amount of game present was "quite substantial" (Gad 1970, 39). The faunal assemblages in Greenland, which contained a plethora of remains of marine animals but a dearth of livestock remains, indicated that the Norse "probably shifted their main dietary reliance from terrestrial to marine foodstuffs" (Lynnerup and Von Wowern 1970, 235). Though grains were rare and domestic animals difficult to keep, the Norse nonetheless managed to survive in the North Atlantic, relying on dairy and marine products.

Such a transition in diet was supported by chemical analysis of bones from the North Farm at Brattahlið. Bone mineral content samples were taken from human skeletons to search for signs of nutritional stress at this new outpost in the North Atlantic and to determine the source of protein intake for its inhabitants. Though BMC measurements can be skewed by post-mortem diagenesis—post-depositional processes affecting the basic bone chemistry—of archaeologically excavated bone, x-rays of the bones analyzed revealed that the samples had been well preserved (Lynnerup and Von Wowern 1970, 237). The study produced two important results: firstly "there was no evident age-related bone loss for either males or females" (Lynnerup and Von Wowern 1970, 236), which suggested a steady dietary intake with no signs of nutritional stress. More important for this discussion, however, is the "substitution of terrestrial with marine protein sources, without an overall increase in protein intake" (Lynnerup and Von Wowern 1970, 238). Thus the difficulties of raising crops and domestic livestock in Greenland led to a decrease on reliance on these farming products, and an increase in consumption of foods from the sea.

Excavations of faunal materials at the Farm Beneath the Sand confirmed this transition to a reliance on marine resources and dairy products. The copious amounts of bones present in the cultural layer of the living spaces provide solid archaeological evidence that the diet of the Greenlanders consisted of few domestic animals. Most of the bones came from wild game—caribou, hare, and seal—which confirmed that "domestic animals were kept for milk or wool" (Berglund 2000, 299). Though few remains of fish bones were present, this was typical for early Norse sites, especially in Greenland. The general scarcity of fish bones in Greenland middens remains a puzzle, given the relative ease with which the inhabitants of Greenland would have been able to fish. Although Greenland had an abundance of cod, trout, and salmon, which were most likely exploited by the initial settlers, it is unlikely that a large amount of faunal evidence would remain, as fish bones are small, easily soluble, and do not preserve well in the archaeological record (Berglund 2000, 299). This scarcity of fish in the Greenland faunal assemblage is in marked contrast to that of similar sites in Iceland, despite Greenland having "conditions of organic preservation far better than found on most Icelandic sites, and recovery strategies that produced substantial collections of insects, hair, and small seeds" (Perdikaris and McGovern 2007, 207). Therefore, it appears that the inhabitants of Greenland did not include fish as a substantial part of their diet.

Dietary Practices at L'Anse aux Meadows
A diet similar to those of Iceland and Greenland would have been highly possible and practical at L'Anse aux Meadows. Wild game can still be found in Newfoundland today, though limited in number. Caribou and black bear numbers have dwindled, but from records of explorers in the end of the 15th century, "we know that the fauna of Newfoundland was unusually rich and varied," and that there were large numbers of reindeer, fox, wolf, lynx, sable, whale, salmon, cod, and seal (A.S. Ingstad 1985a, 25). Ingstad noted that there was such an abundance of flounder in the waters of Épaves Bay that "they can at times, in shallow water, be seen lying packed close like tiles on a roof" (Ingstad and Ingstad 2000, 90). The Ingstads tested a method of catching fish described in the Vinland sagas; they dug trenches into the sand at low tide, and at the next low tide these were filled with fish (Ingstad and Ingstad 2000, 90). Indeed, modern life in Newfoundland relies upon marine food, and "agriculture is of little importance"; instead, the small fishing villages depended (at least until the 1970s) on cod and seals to supplement their economy and diet (A.S. Ingstad 1985a, 25). Seals, in particular, were important, as "the breeding grounds of the Greenland seal lie off the coast of Labrador and the Gulf of St. Lawrence," at which they arrive in September; the breeding season lasts until May, when the seals leave to return to Greenland (A.S. Ingstad 1985a, 26). Thus, the Norse settlers at L'Anse aux Meadows not only would have had access to seal and fish for marine protein, they would have been intimately familiar with their capture.

The scarce evidence of dietary remains at L'Anse aux Meadows suggested that sources of marine foodstuffs—fish and seals—held the dominant position among animal sources of protein. A bone from Room III, Hall D, initially determined by the Ingstads to be from a domestic pig (*Sus scrofa*), was used as evidence that livestock had indeed been kept on the site, as well as to prove the Norse provenance of its inhabitants: "the small, charred fragment of a pig's bone found in house A proves that the people who lived in the house must have had domestic animals: the inhabitants can therefore have been neither Indians nor Eskimos" (A.S. Ingstad 1985c, 180). The Parks Canada investigations, however, demonstrated that the bone belonged not to a pig, but to a seal (*Phoca groenlandica*). The remaining bones found on the site were of other seal species (*Phoca hispida* and *Phoca vitulina*), fish, most likely cod, and whale, which composed 80% of all faunal remains (Wallace 1990, 176). Interpretation of these remains, however, was made difficult by the preservation conditions on the terrace. Only one fishbone—a vertebra "probably from cod"—found in the long hearth of Room III in Hall D, survived only because it was calcified (Wallace 1990, 184); the preservation of whalebone at the site, in contrast, was most likely a result of "differential preservation and original size" (Wallace 1990, 176). Unless the bones had calcified, like the vertebra in Hall D, they would have "rarely survived" in the moderately acidic soils [pH 4.0 to 6.0] at L'Anse aux Meadows; even the seal bones had survived only because of calcification—the only non-calcified bones at the site were the whalebones in Hall F (Wallace 1990, 176).

The scarcity of fish bones on the terrace above Épaves Bay does not indicate that fish were not eaten at the site; the discovery of the birchbark container interpreted as a net-sinker and the possibility of stones as fishing weights suggests that fish were caught, as does comparison with contemporary practices in Iceland. It is more than likely that the inhabitants of L'Anse aux Meadows supplied themselves with the abundant cod which could be caught easily in the bay. In contrast, the lack of larger bones of domestic animals at L'Anse aux Meadows is surprising, considering the abundant presence of such bones at the Farm Beneath the Sand, a comparable—albeit agricultural—settlement, where there was plentiful evidence of dietary practices in the bones "found everywhere in the [cultural] layer" (Berglund 2000, 301). Additionally, as small bone fragments have survived within the soil, the lack of animal teeth—usually a well-preserved category of artifacts—at L'Anse aux Meadows indicates that no domestic animals were butchered there. In comparison with the Farm Beneath the Sand, L'Anse aux Meadows' residents appears not to have consumed livestock. This does not, however, mean that livestock were not brought to Newfoundland for dairy products, simply that there was no evidence of livestock having been butchered on the site.

The paucity of faunal dietary evidence at L'Anse aux Meadows may in great part have resulted from the poor preservation conditions on the sandy terrace. Wallace analyzed the peat bog next to the terrace for the presence of bone and ash, however, "recognizing the fact that bone and ashes might also have been deposited on the bog side of the houses, and that these materials could consequently have been dissolved by the chemicals in the bog" (Wallace 1990, 182). The results of the chemical analyses revealed that ash and bone had never been present in the bog. The lack of faunal remains must be explained in order to fully understand dietary practices at L'Anse aux Meadows, and to conclude whether or not livestock had actually been present on the site. For comparison, Greenland and Iceland provide the closest temporal, geographical, and environmental comparative evidence for the site at L'Anse aux Meadows.

Livestock at L'Anse aux Meadows

As barns and byres in Iceland and Greenland contained double rows of posts in a manner similar to the larger halls, measures must be taken to identify the use of each building at L'Anse aux Meadows that was constructed in such a manner. The best indicator that a structure was a dwelling is the presence of a central hearth within the building; additionally, the use of such a building for keeping livestock could be indicated by the types of organic debris left behind.

Comparisons to contemporary Norse farming sites, already shown to be similar in building construction and layout to L'Anse aux Meadows, indicated that the settlement on Épaves Bay was not a colonizing venture based on farming. At the farms of Jarlshof in Shetland and Havítárholt in Iceland, the longhouse was surrounded with outbuildings (A.S. Ingstad 1985c, 173). House 1C at Jarlshof, one of the outbuildings to the larger *skáli*, was determined to have served as a byre based upon its complete lack of internal features, including hearths, as a result of the 1936 excavations; Jarlshof's last excavator J.R.C. Hamilton wrote that "the absence of such features, particularly hearths, suggests that the building served some menial purpose, such as a barn or byre" (1956, 111) The large complex of farms at Warendorf in Westphalia entails four or five farms, each farm consisting "of a large dwelling house and fourteen or fifteen out-houses"; this settlement exemplified a farm "of the fully developed Norse Viking Age type: one or more large dwelling houses surrounded by a number of outbuildings, each of which served one of the many requirements of the farm" (A.S. Ingstad 1985c, 175). The one or two smaller buildings associated with each hall at L'Anse aux Meadows paled in quantitative comparison.

The difficulty in determining whether or not the inhabitants of L'Anse aux Meadows had livestock lies in the fact that it was not a typical farming settlement, and thus cannot be specifically compared to contemporary farming sites in Iceland and Greenland. As the Norse left Iceland for other places further west in the North Atlantic, they would have searched for areas that permitted them to keep livestock and perhaps grow crops. The initial settlers of Iceland "were intent on establishing permanent farmsteads and a way of life similar to what they knew in their homelands" (Vésteinsson 2000, 171). Having found such areas in Iceland, where the domestic animals they brought with them from Norway—sheep, goats, horses, cattle, swine, dogs, cats, and poultry (Rafnsson 1997, 120)—thrived, it is not inappropriate to imagine that on exploring further west, they would have expected to find similar locations: "places where fodder could be procured before winter fell and where hunting and fishing could be relied on to provide subsistence until the domestic animals had multiplied" (Vésteinsson 2000, 171). The lack of definite barns and byres at L'Anse aux Meadows could thus be explained as the Norse having allowed their sheep and cows graze in the open meadows during a mild winter (A.S. Ingstad 1985d, 263).

Wallace, however, reached a difference conclusion based on the lack of evidence of the keeping of livestock at L'Anse aux Meadows, that "the site had not been a regular Norse settlement based on farming" (Wallace 2000a, 173). Though Parks Canada attempted to locate buildings additional to the three Complexes and Smithy, which could have been used as byres, barns, or enclosures for livestock, "so prevalent on Iceland and Greenland sites," they found none (Wallace 2000a, 173). There were also no bones of domestic animals in the faunal assemblage. If the Norse had brought livestock, they had been "few in number and either consumed or kept outside in the winter" (Wallace 2000a, 173); the dearth of faunal evidence could be explained by either the poor preservation conditions, or by the possibility that any livestock brought for dairy resources were not slaughtered. These absences "made it clear that [L'Anse aux Meadows] had not been a colonising settlement" (Wallace 2000a, 173). Wallace judges that "subsistence was probably not geared to self-sufficiency dependant on livestock or cultivation," with provisions "obtained via hunting, fishing and gathering of local resources" (Wallace 1990, 192).

There are, however, certain buildings at L'Anse aux Meadows that could suggest the presence of livestock. Comparisons of Norse structures suggest that Hut C, the crude hut at the southern end of the terrace, could have been used as a sheep-cote, but there is no conclusive proof of this (A.S. Ingstad 1985d, 263). Similar buildings elsewhere in the North North Atlantic, such as the byres at Brattahlid (85 IMG NS), generally have stone-paved floors when they are indeed used as byres. None of the buildings at L'Anse aux Meadows, however, have stone floors, which eliminates one method of identification.

The drainage ditch in Hall F may indicate that animals were at some point kept indoors, as the ditch could have moved animal filth out of the house and down the terrace: the presence of Room VII at the other end of the ditch makes such a conclusion difficult. However, it must be kept in mind that Room VII was not discovered during the initial Ingstad excavations, and appears not to have any entrances or exits. It is possible that its walls were not originally roofed, and may have in fact been a type of animal enclosure used in conjunction with Room V. In a similar manner, the arms of turf extending from Hut C could also have been used for livestock management, rather than as a protective measure against the flood, as Ingstad originally suggested.

The presence of animal parasites and manure on a site, such as at the Farm Beneath the Sand, can indicate which buildings were used to house livestock (Buckland 2000, 149). Also, at sites such as Ruin Group V52 at Umiviarssuk in Greenland, the floor of a building determined to be a cattle shed "consisted of an irregular layer of flagstones covered by a thick layer of sheep manure" (Albrethsen 2000, 103). At the contemporary site at the bishop's seat of Garðar in Greenland, the wetland conditions of the site allowed the preservation of insect and parasitic evidence for the spreading of manure from (Buckland et. al. 2009, 112). Such secondary faunal material was totally absent at L'Anse aux Meadows, however, despite similar preservation conditions in the bog. In spite of the lack of conclusive evidence that livestock were kept at L'Anse aux Meadows, Ingstad believed it to be "most likely that the Norsemen should have kept domestic animals here at L'Anse aux Meadows," as she wondered "why would they choose to settle at a place with such excellent pasture as Épaves Bay if it were not for their stock?" (A.S. Ingstad 1985d, 263). However, though the inhabitants of the Norse buildings at L'Anse aux Meadows may have eventually intended for the site to become a permanent settlement with livestock, there is no indication that such a transition in settlement pattern ever occurred during its occupation.

There is therefore not enough archaeological evidence to determine whether or not livestock were kept at L'Anse aux Meadows. Since Norse buildings at L'Anse aux Meadows had *not* been intended as a formal settlement, the presence of livestock would not have strictly been necessary: consider the Viking overwintering military settlements, which were built to house the warriors, and not their cattle. If animals were brought along, but kept solely for dairy products, there would be no indication in the faunal record of their presence, though there may be remains of manure or insects. If animals were butchered, the bones may not have survived the last millennium, as preservation conditions on the terrace are so poor; this is unlikely, as seal and whale bones have survived, though this may be a disparity in favor of these species. In this case, therefore, the Vinland settlement model may be consulted to provide an indication as to whether or not livestock may have been kept at L'Anse aux Meadows. Wallace explained that the livestock "must have been left outside during the winter," for "there is no doubt that some animals would have been brought from Greenland to assure that the expedition would have access to milk, butter, and cheese during their long stay, and meat for the return voyage" (Wallace 2006, 58). Use of the Vinland model indicated that livestock could have been brought to L'Anse aux Meadows; the lack of faunal evidence therefore likely results from their use as dairy resources or poor preservation conditions.

Palynological Studies
Palynological analysis indicates that at the time of Norse settlement near the end of the 10th century CE, the vegetation present was not particularly different than in modern times and had not been significantly changed in the centuries beforehand. Pollen analyses and chemical analyses of other organic materials on the site showed that the climate at L'Anse aux Meadows was only slightly warmer during the Norse occupation, with no substantial change in vegetation (Wallace 1990, 170). At the time of excavation, the site and its surrounding area were home to shrubby trees rather than to a "genuine forest," with herbaceous vegetation and heath dominating (Henningsmoen 1985, 314). Grasses and sedges were also present in abundance, and "the area could undoubtedly offer pasture for domestic animals" (Henningsmoen 1985, 315). The vegetation consisted mostly of the following types of plants: sub-arctic heath; bog and muskeg; dwarf forms of balsam fir, spruce, tamarack, birch, alder and willow (Wallace, "1976 Excavations," 1977, 8). Pine, which can be found in the southern part of Newfoundland, does not grow at L'Anse aux Meadows (Bell, Macpherson, and Renouf 2000, 213). Red and black currants, cloudberries, gooseberries, strawberries, and blackberries are also abundant in modern times.

Eight pollen sample series were taken at various distances from the site at L'Anse aux Meadows. These locations were chosen so that the sample could indicate any changes in forestation over the last several thousand years (Henningsmoen 1985, 316). Two were at a distance of more than 10 km from the site, three within a 3 km radius, and three within 100 m from the structures. Through such analyses, any substantial change in vegetation would be visible in the pollen diagrams from either the forest or meadow and bog, or both. "No obvious contamination of the samples was recorded, and no samples had to be rejected owing to suspected contamination" (Henningsmoen 1985, 317). Included in the pollen graphs were Arboreal Pollen (AP), Norarboreal Pollen (NAP), and Entomophilous Herbs (EP), which were included in the pollen sum, as well as Spores and Aquatic plant Pollen (AqP), which were not included in the pollen sum.

Four samples series were also taken from the walls of the turf structures on the terrace above Épaves Bay, so that the origins of the turf material could be studied (Henningsmoen 1985, 316); one sample from the wall separating Rooms I and III in Hall D, one from the northeast wall of Hall F, and two from Hall A, one in the north wall and one in the south. Palynological analysis of the samples from the turf walls of the Norse houses confirmed that the sod used to build them was cut from different locations on the site. All samples were also radiocarbon dated (Henningsmoen 1985, 317). These dates corresponded with the estimated date of the settlement itself, roughly 950 ± 50–90 years B.P. (discussed below)

The sampling sites closest to the archaeological site provided the best data regarding vegetation changes near the settlement. Palsa Bog dates 5320 ± 60 years B.P. (3370 BCE ± 60) at a depth of 170 cm, and dates to 460 ± 80 years B.P. (1490 ± 80 CE) closer to the surface at a depth of 30-35 cm (Henningsmoen 1985, 333). Located in the central area of the peat bog behind the Norse site, this sample can be "assured to register possible vegetational changes at the site;" however, there are no indications that large-scale vegetation change occurred during the Norse occupation (Henningsmoen 1985, 334). The sampling location 30 m east of Hall F, dated to 1480 ± 100 years B.P. (470 ± 100 CE) at a depth of 45–55 cm, was similarly expected to show "vegetational traces of Norse activity," and being closer to the actual habitation zone, was expected to do so "perhaps more clearly than the Palsa Bog locality" (Henningsmoen 1985, 337). However, the diagram for this location as well revealed no traces of the Norsemen either in arboreal exploitation or in agriculture.

All three sample groups—two samples from the forested area 10 km from the site, three samples at no greater distance than 3 km from the site, and the three samples within the site itself—confirmed that no anomalous changes occurred at the time of Norse occupation. There has been no change in forest cover from the period before Norse occupation of the site to the present day, and indeed, the study demonstrated that "no profound vegetation change has taken place during the last c. 7 ½ millennia" (Henningsmoen 1985, 346). In contrast, in Iceland, large-scale clearance of the birch forests "suggests that the earliest settlers were intent on occupying the land completely" (Vésteinsson 2000, 167).

Wallace concluded differently, that the meadows surrounding L'Anse aux Meadows "were not here a thousand years ago when ancient balsam firs, poplars, and larches dominated and a thick snarl of softwood forest and brush edged the site" (Wallace 2000c, 209). However, Ingstad's conclusion that the meadows were present at the end of the first millennium was supported by Kari Henningsmoen's work, which finds "the ratio between herbaceous pollen and tree pollen dating from the time of the Norse settlement to be more or less identical with that of today" (A.S. Ingstad 1985d, 263). Although Ingstad's team had looked for "a conspicuous 'landnam' phase, as seen in the pollen diagrams from Greenland and Iceland," they found none; thus, the Norse occupation at L'Anse aux Meadows had been "too small and too short-lived to leave its mark on the vegetation" (Henningsmoen 1985, 348). The pollen graphs show no indication of a decrease in trees at the site severe enough to allow for deforestation

In contrast to the stability of the pollen record at L'Anse aux Meadows during the time of the Norse arrival is a detailed study of the pollen record at Tasiusaq in Greenland's Eastern Settlement. Prior to the *Landnám* at this site, the pollen graph is dominated by "arboreal and dwarf-shrub" pollens and "high percentages of Cyperacae" (Edwards et. al. 2008, 10); after the arrival of the Norse to the site, however, there is a "rapid (near instantaneous) decline" in birch pollen and an increase in *Poaceae*, implying a clearance of forests and their replacement with grasslands (Edwards et. al. 2008, 10). Similar changes may be seen in the pollen graphs from the contemporary site at Ruin Group Ø34 in the Eastern Settlement, not far from Brattahlið, where elevated *Poaeceae* rates in the post-*landnám* period "are likely to reflect both the establishment of hay fields and an expansion in the area covered by open grassy heath" (Schofield et. al. 2008, 1649). These marked changes in the pollen records of such early settlement sites in Greenland (e.g. Tasiusaq and Ruin Group Ø34) and Iceland (e.g. Svalbarð) are not seen in the pollen records at L'Anse aux Meadows.

The stability of the vegetation at L'Anse aux Meadows presents three main arguments with regard to the dietary possibilities of its Norse inhabitants. Since the plants present at the site have not changed in the last millennium, the edible plants present in modern times—the various types of berries, in particular—would have been available for consumption during the Norse occupation. Similarly, the stability of climate as indicated by the pollen record suggests that the wild game currently present in Newfoundland were probably present during the Norse occupation, allowing the inhabitants to obtain wild game and fish for food. Most important, the continuity of the pollen record indicated that the Norse did not clear large amounts of forest at the time of their settlement, which would be shown by a serious decrease in Arboreal Pollen, and that the bog and meadows were present and well-formed at the time of Norse occupation at the beginning of the eleventh century.

Hearth Evidence and Cooking Structures

The types of hearths used at L'Anse aux Meadows indicated which buildings and rooms were used for cooking and preparing meals. The fireplaces and fire features within the buildings on the site bear great resemblance to one another, and Ingstad attaches "particular importance" to the hearths within the houses (A.S. Ingstad 1985c, 153). Different Scandinavian hearth-types had different functions: the fire-place, or *arinn*, was always kept lit and "was regarded as sacred"; the kitchen-fire, or *eldhús*, was used for cooking (Shetelig and Falk 1978, 322–3). The characteristic features of hearths—charcoal, ashes, and fire-cracked rocks—indicated the presence of fire, used for heat and cooking. The positioning of the hearths must also be considered; some were placed in a corner (e.g, Hall A Rooms III and IV, Hut E, and Hall F room V), up against a wall (e.g. Hall F Room VI), or in the center of the floor (e.g, House B and Hall F Room II) (A.S. Ingstad 1985c, 153). All three halls, A, D, and F, had in one or more rooms a central or composite long hearth, which is "a centrally located fireplace for cooking and lighting, containing three separate elements: a stone hearth for an open fire, a cooking pit and an ember pit where glowing embers could be kept alive overnight" (Wallace 1990, 179). In contrast, the smaller structures, B, C, E, and G, placed their fireplaces against a wall (Wallace 1990, 179).

Typically, the cooking pits within the buildings were "simple pits dug down into the floor" (A.S. Ingstad 1985c, 153). As is obvious, though, there were several different types of hearths at L'Anse aux Meadows. The simplest was "no more than a fire patch with a layer of charcoal and ashes of varying depth," such as the hearths in Hall A Room II and Hall F Room I (up against the wall), Hall D Room II (in a corner), and House B (in the middle of the floor) (A.S. Ingstad 1985c, 153). Such a variance in the positioning indicates that "there seems to have been no hard and fast rule about the position of fire patches" (A.S. Ingstad 1985c, 153). A second hearth type "consists of an oval, elongated depression in the floor, which runs in the longitudinal direction of the room, and has no surrounding stone setting," such as those of Hall A Rooms I, II, III, and IV, Hall D Room III, and Hall F Rooms I and II; the placement of hearths of this sort within the larger halls and not within the smaller houses may be indicative of the ways in which they were used (A.S. Ingstad 1985c, 153–4).

The buildings on the terrace also contained several distinctly unique hearths, most of which are found in Hall F; thus, the hearths of Hall F deserve a more in-depth comparison. The hearth in Hut E, also a chambered hearth bounded by a stone slab and lying in a corner, differed only from that of Room IV in Hall F in that it had only one chamber (A.S. Ingstad 1985c, 154). Room IV of Hall F contained its two-chambered stone-lined hearth placed against a corner wall, which was "without parallels in the other houses" (A.S. Ingstad 1985c, 154). Hearths of this type were "quite common in Greenland," and could have up to three compartments (A.S. Ingstad 1985c, 219). The long hearth in Room III, similarly to shallower, elongated central hearth in Room I, lacked evidence "to suggest that food had been prepared here [in either hearth]," and instead they were most likely used "exclusively as sources of heat and light" (A.S. Ingstad 1985c, 215). Cooking pits were present in Rooms II, V, and VI of Hall F, and were similar to those in Hall A and House B (A.S. Ingstad 1985c, 215). Of particular interest, Room II's elongated tripartite hearth was of a type common to other Norse sites, but otherwise lacking at L'Anse aux Meadows: a flat, burnt slab of stone, a cooking pit, and an ember pit (A.S. Ingstad 1985c, 154). Such a hearth, particularly the large stone slab, was used in Greenland during the early settlement period (A.S. Ingstad 1985c, 219). The slab "may have been used for baking a kind of unleavened bread" by lighting a fire on top of the stone to heat it, then sweeping the stone clean for baking (A.S. Ingstad 1985c, 217).

Remains of meals were found within and around some of the hearths. Charred bone fragments were found in several hearths and features throughout the site: the midden between Rooms I and II in Hall A; the midden outside Room II, Hall A; the northwest corner hearth in Room III, Hall A; the cooking pit in House B; the long hearth and ember pit of Room III, Hall D; the cultural layer in Room II, Hall F; the hearths in Rooms V and VI, Hall F; and the midden between Rooms VI and III, outside of Hall F. This indicated that food was cooked in Rooms I, II, and III of Hall A; House B; Room III of Hall D; and Rooms II, V, and VI of Hall F. The fat in the cultural layers of Rooms I, II and V of Hall F indicates that some sort of animal was butchered within Hall F, as this fat could only come from an animal.

Norse Diet at L'Anse aux Meadows
Palynological analyses indicate that the climate at L'Anse aux Meadows has not changed since the time of Norse occupation, indicating both that the Norse did not practice large-scale agriculture and that they had access to the same types of plants that grow in Newfoundland today. This lack of large-scale agriculture confirms that L'Anse aux Meadows was not a long-term settlement based on farming; thus, L'Anse aux Meadows must be compared to Wallace's Vinland settlement model to determine dietary habits, particularly as the faunal record is so poor. The inhabitants of the site prepared and cooked their food over the cooking pits within buildings A, B, D, and F. The inhabitants relied on marine sources of fish and seal meat, and though there is no conclusive archaeological evidence for such, may have kept the minimal number of livestock to fulfill the dairy requirements of their diet.

CHAPTER 5 Site Occupation and Social Analysis

This final chapter considers the questions of who lived at the site and from where they came. Site dating shows that L'Anse aux Meadows was inhabited at the turn of the first millennium, the time at which the Vinland sagas recount that voyages to this region occurred, further arguing for the use of the Vinland settlement model to determine the social structure of this atypical Norse outpost. The use of the Vinland model allows the calculation of the amount of people occupying the site and a comparative data set with which to determine the social structure at L'Anse aux Meadows, both of which are more difficult to understand without such a comparison. Finally, analysis of the nineteen fist-sized stones in relation to the 'post holes' in Hut E indicates a female presence in the site via the identification of weaving as a site activity.

Radiocarbon Dating

Samples for radiocarbon dating were taken by both the Ingstads and by Parks Canada. The two teams were able to gather "one of the highest number of radiocarbon dates determined for any site in the world at that time" (Wallace 2000a, 168): the Ingstads took 22, and Wallace took 118, for a total of 140 dates, "at the time when five or six dates per site was often considered sufficient" (Wallace 2000a, 168).

Radiocarbon analysis of wood scraps and charcoal revealed dates that fall into four main chronological groups. The first was from the Maritime Archaic, c. 1000–700 BCE. The second was based on cut wood pieces, dated to 600–700 CE. The third, to which the Norse settlement appears to belong, centered around 1000 CE. The last, based mainly on wood twigs from Hall D, dated to 1350–1600 CE (Wallace, "1976 Excavations," 1977, 2). Many of the dates from the second group came from charcoal samples from both within and outside of the Norse buildings, the discrepancy of which is startling. Much of Ingstad's and Wallace's discussion of dates has been on the interpretation of a feature which contains separate dates of both the 11th and 14th centuries CE. However, several factors must be kept in mind when considering the interpretation.

Firstly, dates from two separate chronological groupings can be found within the same building, from samples taken both during the Ingstad and the Wallace excavations. From the Ingstad excavations, three samples were taken from Hall A. All were from charcoal samples, yet all yield disparate dates: 950 ± 90, 1000 CE; 1320 ± 80, 630 CE; 1310 ± 130, 640 CE. Two fall into the second chronological grouping, while one falls into that of the presumed Norse occupation. House F, where four samples were dated, shows such a similar grouping: from the turf wall itself, 950 ± 50, 1000 CE; from a piece of whalebone in Room III, 925 ± 1000, 1025 CE; from charcoal in Rooms II and IV, respectively, 1080 ± 70, 870 CE, and 1250 ± 70, 700 CE. The Smithy, also, has disparate dates, from two samples of charcoal; 1090 ± 90, 860 CE, and 890 ± 70, 1060 CE. Many of the dates cluster around the eighth century CE, but the dates range from 440–780 CE to 1020–1310 CE. Each date was tree-ring calibrated and there was a 95% probability within two standard deviations that the dates are correct (Wallace 1990, 180). Thus, the disparity between the groups of dates is real, and could either indicate an occupation of the site from the fifth to the fourteenth century, or several distinct occupations, neither of which agrees with the archaeological analysis (Wallace 1990, 180).

These discrepancies have been explained in two ways. Ingstad suggested that the material used for fuel and building during the beginning of the settlement was most likely the extensive quantities of driftwood present on the shore of Épaves Bay. Thus, the radiocarbon dates obtained from wood of this type would assuredly pre-date the site occupation (A.S. Ingstad 1985d, 255–6). Wallace agreed that the age of the wood used at L'Anse aux Meadows "could severely skew the dates"; such discrepancies have occurred at early sites in Iceland, where the radiocarbon dates pre-dated the colonization period by several centuries (Wallace 1990, 181). The second explanation is that the sample from an artifact or feature submitted for radiocarbon analysis was taken from the center of the tree; as some trees, such as spruce, can live for five hundred to a thousand years, the heartwood of such trees would of course date to a much earlier time than the year in which it was cut down (Wallace 2006, 71). Either scenario is possible.

Wallace found significant the fact that seven young branches and twigs agree on a mean date of 990–1050 CE (Wallace 2006, 72); the addition of mass spectrometer-accelerated dates prove the mean date of the site to be roughly 980–1020 CE (Wallace 1990, 182). Of the samples taken during the Ingstad excavations, none of the dates obtained from charcoal samples dated beyond 1100 CE; both early and late dates occurred within the same feature, which indicates that the event which formed the feature was no younger than the youngest date. Thus, these youngest twigs, which unlike some of the longer-lived trees cannot have existed for very long, provided the more accurate dates for the site; and when found in a feature, the older dates of the charcoal must be set aside in favor of the younger dates of the twigs and branches.

Similar results have been found in radiocarbon dating of an early farm in Reykjavík, in Iceland. Though in this case the series of samples were "spatially coherent," they were also "statistically distinct" (Smith 1995, 325): the first, dating to the sixth century, came from driftwood on a lake beach deposit; the second, from the late eighth century, came from burnt charcoal beneath the walls of the site structure; and the third, dating to the ninth- to eleventh-centuries, came from cultural layers within the buildings (Smith 1995, 325). In contrast, the site at Reykjavík is historically dated to the later ninth century. In a manner similar to Wallace's interpretation of the radiocarbon dates at L'Anse aux Meadows, the radiocarbon dates from Reykjavík in comparison to building analysis suggested that the site had been inhabited in the ninth century, but that pieces of driftwood from earlier centuries had been used as fuel. In light of this evidence, Wallace's conclusions concerning the dating of L'Anse aux Meadows are convincing.

Architectural Evidence: Occupation Date and Length

The comparative dating of artifacts has already been discussed (Chapter 3). Wallace also used site construction methods and relative dating to place the founding of L'Anse aux Meadows firmly within the late 10th–early 11th century. The architecture implies that the site must have been built:

a) shortly before stone foundations became common, and before separate pit buildings and central, composite longfires went out of use, and;
b) shortly after side annexes and other additional rooms became customary and interior walls of sod, a centrally-placed entrance, and wall hearths were common. (Wallace 1990, 179).

The most likely time for all of these characteristics to have coincided, according to Wallace, was the early eleventh century.

The length of habitation at L'Anse aux Meadows must also be deduced. The stratigraphy of the site unequivocally demonstrated that "the Norse occupation had been one single, short-lived episode" (Wallace 2000a, 168). The cultural layer of the site is relatively thin and the shallow depth of the middens on the terrace is indicative of a short-term stay; the largest midden at L'Anse aux Meadows was 3 to 4 m wide by 25 cm deep, while those outside of Halls A, D, and F were no more than 1 m^2 and 3–10 cm deep (Wallace 1990, 182). In contrast, the midden at the Niaqussat site in the West Settlement of Greenland, which was occupied for 350 years, had garbage deposits 150 m long and 1.7 m deep (Wallace 2000a, 169). Though post-depositional processes may account for partial erosion of the middens at L'Anse aux Meadows, they are certainly much shallower than their cousins in Greenland and Iceland. Furthermore, the middens contain no more than a few small fragments of animal bone, and no other indicators of diet. Additionally, and perhaps most noticeably for a medieval Norse site, there were no cemeteries or graves at L'Anse aux Meadows. Though burials could have disintegrated in the acidic terrace, there was no evidence at all that the soil had been disturbed for inhumation (Wallace 1990, 183).

Building construction techniques also indicate that the site was inhabited for a short period of time. In comparison with other Norse sites, the lack of stone foundations at L'Anse aux Meadows, combined with the "flimsy proportions" of some of the walls on the site indicate that the houses were "erected with some haste and not intended for long-term occupation" (Schonback et. al. 1976, 11). The short period of integrity of the Norse turf buildings—roughly 50 years—confirms the above analyses in showing that L'Anse aux Meadows was "a short-lived settlement, probably only a decade or so, from *c.* AD [CE] 1000," particularly as there is no indication that the buildings were ever repaired (Wallace 2000a, 177; Gad 1970, 37). Short-term habitation was also shown in the relative lack of artifact evidence. Though the buildings were most likely abandoned in an orderly fashion, with "the owners taking their belongings with them as they left," the lack of domestic artifacts suggests that there were few present at the beginning of the settlement (Wallace 2000a, 177). Those few that were left behind were "either small personal things that had been lost during the stay, such as a bronze pin, the spindle whorl, the bead, and the needle hone, or things that were broken or discarded" (Wallace 2000c, 214).

Locations such as the one occupied by the L'Anse aux Meadows site in Greenland and Iceland were *avoided* for *permanent* settlements (Wallace 1990, 189); the area lacks inland waterways, exploration to the south was barred by impenetrable forests and marshes, and there was "no potential for communication between the L'Anse aux Meadows area and the interior" (Wallace 1990, 189). Thus, the site was "uncharacteristic of permanent West Norse settlements where internal contact between farms by water *and* land were a prerequisite for social cohesion" (Wallace 1990, 189). The placement of the buildings on the terrace above Épaves Bay thus suggests in itself that L'Anse aux Meadows was not intended to be permanent, though there were advantages to its location for an expeditionary base camp: easy access to open water, inhabitable land close to the shore, and an agreeable climate.

Population Size

The number of people who lived at L'Anse aux Meadows can be determined by calculations based upon the size of each building, and by comparison with other Norse sites. Sufficient knowledge of Norse Viking Age site populations and room functions exists to calculate the probable capacity of each turf structure on the terrace at Épaves Bay, particularly in regards to the amount of sleeping space available. As the actual size of sleeping platforms at L'Anse aux Meadows is unknown because of poor preservation, the calculations must be based on the amount of floor space that the inhabitants would have needed to construct beds. Beds typically measured 1.8 m in length, and were wide enough to allow two people to sleep side-by-side. The amount of floor space in the turf buildings according to Wallace's calculations suggested the following populations for each residence: Hall A, 30; House B, 2–3; Hall D, 24; and Hall F: 38. Had Houses C, E, and G also included sleeping space, they would have allowed for 1–3 people each. Thus, the minimum estimate for the site is 94–95, while the maximum is 96–104 (Wallace 1990, 188).

The above calculations assumed that L'Anse aux Meadows operated with all houses inhabited at once. However, the site "probably did not operate with a full complement of occupants for more than about half of the year" (Wallace 1990, 188). Thus, the site would need to provide for a maximum of roughly one hundred people, but at any given time was most likely occupied by fewer than that, probably between thirty and sixty, depending on the number of halls occupied at one time. Such a settlement pattern closely resembles the Viking military camp at Steigen in Norway, which "was probably not occupied much more than two weeks at a time" (Wallace 1990, 188). Given the similar temporary nature of each site, it was logical to compare a calculation of residence population based on the Steigen model to that calculated based on L'Anse aux Meadows itself, as Wallace did.

Steigen was excavated and analyzed by Johansen and Søbstad, who computed that the houses at Steigen could shelter at maximum 20 people each, "basing their figure on a requirement of 2 m^2 per person" (Wallace 1990, 188). This figure, however, was based on the practical density of population in a military camp, and that 10 people per house would be a more comfortable and reasonable estimate. Wallace calculated, according to the Steigen model and based on the amount of space in the living areas of the houses at L'Anse aux Meadows the amount of people who could conceivably live in each building at one time; the estimates are: Hall A, 37; Hall D: 31, Hall F: 40, and Hall B: 4; Total, 112 (Wallace 1990, 188). Both the calculations based solely on L'Anse aux Meadows and the calculations based on the Steigen model thus suggest that a hundred people could occupy the site at any one time, though occupation may not have been at full capacity throughout the period of habitation.

Social Structure

Questions regarding who actually occupied these houses still remain: Who were they? Where did they come from? Who led the group, and how did it function?

The archaeological assemblages provided little information about the inhabitants of the site. The occupants were undoubtedly Norse, as has been identified through architectural and artifact evidence. Their starting location may be derived from feature and artifact evidence. The Icelandic and Greenland origin of the inhabitants of L'Anse aux Meadows has already been discussed above.

The buildings "give an indication of [economic and social] differentiation": Wallace suggested that the large Halls A, D and F at L'Anse aux Meadows have parallels with those on large Norse farms which were occupied by the elite, while the smaller buildings B, C, E and G would have occupied by less socially important peoples at a typical Norse settlement site (Wallace 1990, 187). Thus, the buildings "reveal that not everyone on the site was equal" (Wallace 2000c, 212). There is no doubt that L'Anse aux Meadows had a single central authority; in order for the site to function as it did, with its activities resulting in useful products, the site needed an effective social coordination (Wallace 1990, 191). Of the Halls, F may have housed the leader of the expedition to L'Anse aux Meadows and his crew, as it was the "largest and most complex, and its living quarters showed a more intensive use, with more artifacts and occupation refuse than the corresponding rooms in the south hall [D]" (Wallace 2000c, 212). The third and southern Hall A, which lacked a private chamber, "was probably used as quarters for a third crew, perhaps hired especially for the expedition" (Wallace 2000c, 213).

At least three relatively wealthy people lived at the site: no one else would have had the resources to build three boats, hire three crews, and sail into the west on an expedition. The scant artifact evidence confirmed this hypothesis of wealth, with the small bead of glass—an expensive material—and the copper-alloy ring-pin. The presence of subordinate workers or slaves was also suggested by the lack of specialized activity within the smaller houses (Wallace 2000c, 212), which suggests that they were used for sleeping space for less affluent or socially connected people, who would have otherwise been housed in the sleeping space in the larger halls. Their presence would have been necessary on a site that revolved around chores typically done by such workers or slaves in the eleventh century: charcoal manufacture, processing of bog ore, clearing of the land, and cutting of sod (Wallace 1990, 187). Given the temporary nature of the site, however, it is unclear whether or not these lower-status people would have been simple workers or slaves—would the latter have been trusted in such an unfamiliar environment?

The social structure of the group itself is difficult to analyze from archaeological remains, as there are few actual artifacts on the site; artifacts that could indicate the status of their owners, such as clothes, weapons, and jewelry, are absent. The sagas state who voyaged to Vinland, and thus could be used to fill a large gap in the archaeological record. According to the sagas, the Norse site at L'Anse aux Meadows was occupied by three crews of men from Greenland and Iceland. In such a case, in which text-aided archaeology would typically rely on historical documents, the question of the validity and historicity of the Vinland Sagas becomes a challenge.

Women at L'Anse aux Meadows
The most puzzling question raised, however, is the presence of women at the site. Since the site was atypical—an exploratory outpost practicing no traditional methods of agriculture and without overwhelming evidence of any activity beyond that of smithing and carpentry work—would women have been necessary at such a site?

In traditional Norse Viking Age society, a woman had very specific and structured tasks to perform as part of daily life. In Iceland in particular, "her duties were entirely confined to the farm, where she had great authority," and where she was to assume a well-defined feminine role in the household (Sawyer 2000, "Women," 299). In the settlement in Greenland, in the wilderness on the outskirts of the known world, she was "responsible for many different kinds of work on the farm," where she was required to cook, raise children, spin and weave cloth for clothes and sails, sew skins and furs into clothing, care for cattle, and many of the other tasks necessary for daily life (Ingstad and Ingstad 2000, 16).

Wallace concluded that at L'Anse aux Meadows, "there is little evidence of domestic activities and certainly no indication of normal family life" (Wallace 2000c, 212). Wallace and the Ingstads believed that a small number of women were indeed present at L'Anse aux Meadows, based upon the artifact evidence—the spindle whorl, the bone needle, and the needle hone—in conjunction with the saga evidence that Leif Erikson's men brought their wives with them on the voyage to Vinland. Wallace acknowledged that "male crew members usually provided their own food and did their own cooking on voyages," but argued that since "a fairly lengthy stay was contemplated" for the Vinland voyages, it would therefore be "logical that a few women would have been included" (Wallace 1990, 167). Remembering the careful construction of the several different types of hearths within the buildings, however, it appears as though there may have been some domestic habits at the site after all.

Ingstad proposed Room VI of Hall F as women's quarters based upon the artifacts found within: the spindle whorl and the needle hone. The latter provides little evidence of activity, other than the fact that needles would have been sharpened on the site. Needle hones such as this one, made of quartzite, "are very common in the Norse cultural complex" (A.S. Ingstad 1985c, 226), and were often included in women's sewing kits (Wallace 1990, 187). This needle hone, in combination with the bone needle found on the floor of Hall D in Room VI, suggested that the inhabitants of the site were sewing. The spindle whorl indicated the presence of women at L'Anse aux Meadows, as spinning was a female occupation in Norse society (Wallace 1977, "Norse," 5). Ingstad argued that the find of the needle hone and spindle whorl "would seem to indicate that this was the women's room, and this may be the explanation of the position of room VI in front of the house. This would give the women a more pleasant room in which to work, facing the sun and sheltered from the coldest winds" (A.S. Ingstad 1985c, 214).

It must be remembered, however, that Room VI of Hall F also contained an abundance of iron pieces, and was a room devoted to the repair of ships. The likelihood that women's quarters were in the same room as such labor-intensive work is low. More probable is that the men who were working in Room VI were the ones using the needle. Such a situation is not impossible, and would make sense if L'Anse aux Meadows is indeed an outpost. Men on an exploratory mission would not only need to be able to work with thread, but would need to know how to mend their clothes and the sails of their ships. Such skills would be absolutely essential to the success of an exploration that would undoubtedly take many months. Without the ability to repair torn sails, the men would not get very far in their ships.

Women and Weaving in the Norse North Atlantic
Norse women often had their own rooms within the farm complex. In Iceland and Scandinavia, one of the several sunken-floored huts (*dyngja*) typically found on a farm was usually used for women's work (Ingstad and Ingstad 2000, 165). Stories of the 10th and 11th centuries mention "bowers", separate buildings which served as women's quarters for needlework (Jóhannesson 2006, 340). In the early years of their construction, *dyngja* were placed "at a distance from the other houses, or at least without any direct connection to these," and often lay to the south of the main dwelling, "so that it might be warmed by the sun, while it was at the same time protected from the prevailing winds" (A.S. Ingstad 1985c, 207). Within their quarters, the women would spin, weave or do needlework, all of which activities require specific and easily identifiable tools. The spinning of raw wool into thread to be woven or sewn required: a distaff (*rokkr*), which held the raw material, and a spindle and its whorl (*snaelda*), which in dropping to the floor and being spun would twist the raw material into a yarn (Shetelig and Falk 1978, 333). Occasionally, a simple plaiting of threads with a pair of needles produced *sprang* fabric, which could be used either as a decorative border or as a central piece of fabric (Shetelig and Falk 1978, 333–4).

Weaving was accomplished by means of a large loom, which leaned against the wall or roof-beam (Fig. 5.1). The Icelandic word for the warp-weighted loom, *vetstaður*, translates as both 'stone-weight loom' and 'weaving place' (Østergård 2004, 53).These large looms were heavy, and the wooden posts with which they were created often left marks in the soil floor beneath. The sunken floor provided enough vertical space within the *dyngja* to allow for the height of the loom. The shaft (*skapt*) raised and lowered the vertical warp-threads as the horizontal woof-thread was passed through, and stones (*klé*) hanging at the bottom of the loom kept the warp-threads taut (Shetelig and Falk 1978, 334–5). The warp threads were held taught by rows of stones tied to their ends, in order to keep an evenly distributed tension. Many wooden pieces were used in the weaving process, to keep the threads in place. A large number of warp-weights have been found at sites in Greenland, the majority made of soapstone, as "this material is easy to bore or cut holes in and to adapt so that the stones will have more or less the same weight" (Østergård 2004, 54). These holes were either drilled in the center of the stone or towards the top.

Fig. 5.1, Faroese warp-weighted loom (After Østergård 2004, p 54)

Weaving was specifically a female task, and one of the traditional fabrics woven was called *vaðmal*, a tight, almost waterproof wool cloth that was an important product in Greenland and Icelandic economies (Wallace 2006, 68). In particular, as "textile work was clearly a female responsibility," shipmasters "must have had the support of women to sail" (Christensen 2000, 94).

Typical Norse sites in the North Atlantic yield a great number of artifacts associated with women, and the quarters where women worked were clearly indicated by the artifact assemblage. Quite a few bone needles (Fig. 5.2) were excavated at the Jarlshof farm in Shetland, and in the Norse farm ruins of Greenland (Fig. 5.3) (A.S. Ingstad 1985c, 200). At Brattahlið several broken and intact spindle whorls were discovered, "indicating that women worked here at their spinning-wheels" (Gad 1970, 44). The fact that women's artifacts are clearly found at typical Norse farmsteads in the North Atlantic makes their relative absence at L'Anse aux Meadows remarkable. The scanty artifact assemblage at L'Anse aux Meadows has been interpreted as proof that women were, in fact, present on the site. As the entire site is atypical, however, such a deviance from the normal Norse pattern of women's work would not be surprising, if women were indeed at the site.

Archaeological evidence of weaving has been found at the Farm Beneath the Sand. In its "weaving room" were roughly eighty small stones used as warp weights as well as wooden tools (Fig. 5.4a and 5.4b), along with two beams from the upright loom "on which one can see the marks the warp had cut in the course of time". Also within this room was a hearth constructed of flat stones set on their edges to form a box, built up against a wall; this hearth could be moved, and "thus was not an architectural fixture but an item of furniture" (Berglund 2000, 300). The floor of the room was set half a meter below the floors of the other rooms, suggesting an allowance for the height of a large, warp-weighted loom in the building's construction; this room also contained textile implements and fragments, as well as loom weights (Østergård 2004, 18).

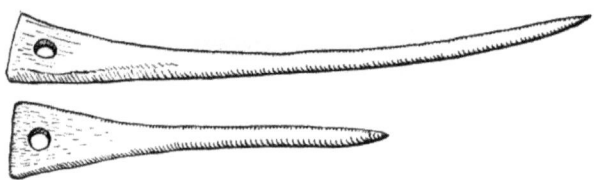

Fig. 5.2, Bone needles from Jarlshof (After Hamilton 1956, 147)

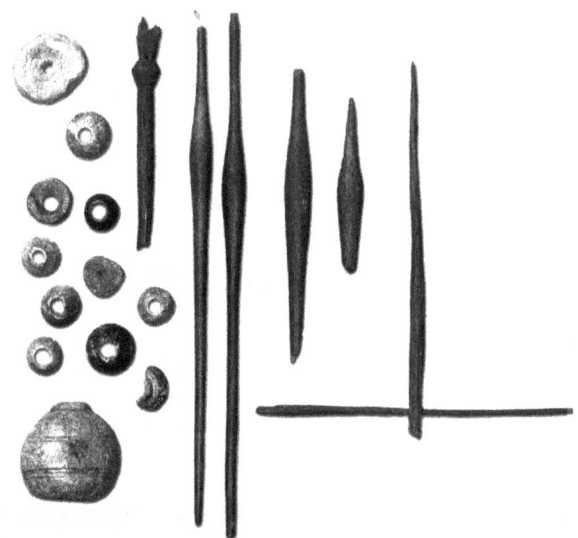

Fig. 5.3, Spindle whorls of soapstone and spindles of wood from farms in the Western Settlement of Greenland. (After Østergård 2004, p 48)

Weaving in Hut E

Conclusive evidence can be found in the archaeological record that at least one woman was present at L'Anse aux Meadows, without reliance on the sagas or the spindle whorl in Hall F. Though Wallace remarks upon the "particularly striking" absence of loom weights at the site, given their common presence on West Norse sites, the nineteen stones found in Hut E may have been used loom weights (Wallace 1990, 187). They could also, however, have been used as fishing weights. Raw data on the loom stones, e.g., their weight, size, etc., would be helpful in determining their use. Ingstad's report, however, does not include the stones in the artifact catalog, nor are they photographed or described in any detail. Thus, the only way to definitively determine whether or not they were used as loom weights is to find evidence of a large loom; given the preservation of post holes in the ground from the wooden posts used to support roofs at L'Anse aux Meadows, a heavy wooden object such as a Norse loom should be expected to leave imprints in the soil of Hut E.

Fig. 5.4a, Spinning and twining hook of wood, found in the Farm Beneath the Sand. The long, thick, and formed stick measures 460 mm, while the short, thin stick measures 160 mm (After Østergård 2004, 49).

Fig. 5.4b, Loom weights from the Farm Beneath the Sand (After Østergård 2004, 55)

When compared with the large assemblage of weaving artifacts and features at the Farm Beneath the Sand, the heap of stones, the two small post holes, and the hearth in Hut E of L'Anse aux Meadows suggest that weaving was done in this small building. The hearth in Hut E was positioned up against the wall, protected by an upright slate slab; the depth of fire debris within this hearth, as mentioned in Chapter 2, was significantly shallower than others of a similar size on the site, barely extending into the floor level. Thus, the hearth in Hut E resembles the movable hearth of the weaving room in the Farm Beneath the Sand. The nineteen stones have already been discussed by Ingstad and Wallace as possible warp weights, but have not been analyzed. Though they are made of limestone and not soapstone, limestone has the same desirable properties as soapstone: easily carved and easy to adapt the create a matching set. It would also be interesting to see whether the pieces of wood recovered by Parks Canada may have been tools used in weaving on a large loom; though the artifact catalog has not been published, some of the pieces of carpentry 'debitage' may in fact be weaving tools such as those found in Greenland.

The two post holes from Ingstad's excavations provide clues indicating that Hut E was used for weaving work. While Ingstad reported on and recorded the two small post holes in Hut E, Wallace did not mention them. In contrast to the larger and more solid post holes surrounding the long central hearths in Halls A, D, and F, it did not appear that the post holes in Hut E actually contained posts nor held up the roof. It is more likely that Hut E had a corbelled roof similar to that of Hut C, as Ingstad initially suggested. If this were case, there would have been no practical architectural purpose for the two post holes in Hut E. However, if a large vertical warp-weighted loom had been used in this Hut, as is suggested by the parallel to the Farm Beneath the Sand, then it is likely that the large poles leaning against a wall to form part of the structure of a loom, as discussed above, could have left behind marks similar to post holes in the floor of the hut. Such marks would not have been as permanent as post holes, and most likely would have disappeared once excavated. This is in direct contrast to the discovery by the Parks Canada team of a post hole in Room IV of Hall F which had gone unnoticed by the Ingstads; clearly, post holes were capable of surviving between excavations, so if the 'post holes' in Hut E were indeed such, they should be expected to survive as well.

It may be concluded, therefore, that Ingstad's "post holes" in Hut E were actually depressions created through the presence and use of a warp-weighted upright loom. When taken into consideration with the hearth and nineteen stones also present in the Hut, this is further evidence that weaving—women's work in the Norse culture—was being done in Hut E. Material remains, rather than recourse to the Vinland settlement model or sagas alone, indicate the presence of women—at the very least, one woman—at L'Anse aux Meadows.

CONCLUSION

The Norse site at L'Anse aux Meadows was not a typical agricultural settlement. The layout of the buildings and the lack of outbuildings to be used in the manner of a typical farm—such as stables, byres, etc.—indicate that "the settlement at L'Anse aux Meadows was not a colonizing, self-sustaining venture depending on farming for its livelihood" (Wallace 2000c, 212). At L'Anse aux Meadows, there is no evidence of agriculture or animal husbandry. There are no definitive barns or byres for the keeping of livestock, and the arrangement of buildings on the terrace indicates that L'Anse aux Meadows did not follow the typical North Atlantic Norse farm pattern, with several outbuildings enclosing a field that could be used for pasturage or crop growth. Archaeological evidence in comparison with settlement patterns, suggests, however, that the Norse may have brought the minimal livestock required for dairy resources.

The site at L'Anse aux Meadows lacks several key components that were typically found at long-term Norse settlements. The absence of each of these features indicates that the settlement on Épaves Bay was intended to be used short-term. Had the settlers intended for L'Anse aux Meadows to be a permanent colony, they most likely would have used some of the larger stones from the shoreline—less than 70 km from the terrace—in the foundations of the turf-wall construction. Thus, their absence may indicate that the turf walls were not intended to be as permanent as the structures in Greenland and Iceland. Additionally, as a Norse turf building typically does not survive for more than 50 years, and no repairs are evident in the *strengur* construction at L'Anse aux Meadows, the buildings were not used for a long period of time.

Most important, the pollen analysis of the levels corresponding with the Norse occupation indicates that the settlement was short-lived. The Norse practiced slash-and-burn agriculture in order to grow crops—a process that leaves a significant dent in the palynological record; similarly, their animal husbandry practices are usually destructive towards nearby woodlands. There may have been small, home-field gardens to provide the settlers with basic necessities, but large-scale farming, which would indicate long-term settlement, did not occur at L'Anse aux Meadows. This can be determined with the absence of any impact on local vegetation around Épaves Bay.

L'Anse aux Meadows lacks evidence of a strong female presence during the Norse occupation; rather, it comprised mainly men "who gathered together for strength, rest and recreation during the winter months, preparing for lucrative attacks—or trading ventures—pursued during the rest of the year" (Wallace 2006, 74). The nineteen stones and marks left by an upright weaving loom in Hut E, however, indicate the presence of a women at L'Anse aux Meadows. A loom would allow for the weaving of textiles for both cloth and ship sails.

The three halls at L'Anse aux Meadows—buildings A, D, and F—had three uses. Most important, they served as living quarters for the inhabitants of the site; they contained cultural deposits with small artifacts and small quantities of food remains, possessed central hearths, and probably once had raised benches along the side walls. Each Hall had its own workshop area and specialty: Hall A focused on smithing, as demonstrated in the large, shallow pit used for forging and the pieces of iron found in Room III; Hall D was used for carpentry work, evidenced by the carpentry debris immediately outside Room II, in the peat bog; and Hall F was used for the necessary tasks for boat repair, particularly Room VI, which contained large quantities of slag and nails. Each building contained storage space for resources. The camp smelted and forged its own iron from the surrounding bog, enabling ship repair in Newfoundland rather than relying solely on materials from Greenland. Ecological and palynological analyses show that at the time of Norse arrival, Newfoundland's temperate climate allowed for a number of resources; floral, faunal, and arboreal. Archaeological evidence indicates that at the turn of the first millennium, the Norse site at L'Anse aux Meadows operated as a short-lived, temporary settlement based not on agriculture, but on exploration.

In conclusion, L'Anse aux Meadows was occupied by roughly 60 to 100 people at the turn of the first millennium. Several had significant social and economic means, or so the artifact and anthropological evidence suggests, particularly the use of large ships for transport. Artifacts and building construction also indicate that some of the settlers were from Greenland, while others were from Iceland, or that a blended culture resulted from adaptations and of a migratory lifestyle. Comparison with the Vinland model confirms much of this archaeological analysis. Artifact evidence and activity debris provides detailed insight into the necessary tasks at L'Anse aux Meadows. Carpentry and iron-working debris, in conjunction with the small huts along the bay interpreted as boat-sheds, as well as the weaving done in Hut E, point to the site's ship repair, and the abundance of such evidence is "the most evident activity in the archaeological record" (Wallace 2000a, 173). Such work would be necessary if further exploration along the North

Atlantic coast were to be undertaken. Some activities may be conclusively deduced from the archaeological data. The production of iron and the subsequent boat repair at L'Anse aux Meadows had not been planned, but were undertaken as necessity dictated.

Acknowledgements

This publication has its origins in my undergraduate thesis written at Boston University. Many people have made this study possible, and I thank them for all of their support in its writing. First and foremost, Dr. Mary Beaudry (Boston University), for her guidance, input, and constructive criticism, and for all of her support in the endeavor of bringing the manuscript to publication. I am indebted to Ms. Loretta Decker and Dr. Birgitta Wallace (Parks Canada) for providing me with site reports and documents, without which this study would have been impossible. Dr. Ksenija Borojevic and Dr. Francisco Estrada-Belli (Boston University) were instrumental in reviewing this study and providing me with an outside perspective. I must also thank Kevin P. Smith (Brown University), for meeting with me to discuss my work and suggesting further research. Finally, I am very grateful to Dr. Robin Fleming (Boston College) for her consideration and direction in preparing the manuscript.

Many thanks to all of my family and friends for tolerating the constant discussion of my research; especially to Amanda Johnson (William & Mary) and Rebecca Mountain (University of Arizona), for their patience and encouragement.

Bibliography

Albrethson, Svend E. "The Early Norse Farm Buildings in Western Greenland: Archaeological Evidence." *Vínland Revisited: The Norse World at the Turn of the First Millennium, Selected papers from the Viking Millennium International Symposium, Sept. 15-24, Newfoundland and Labrador.* Ed. Shannon Lewis-Simpson. St. John's: Historic Sites Association of Newfoundland and Labrador, Inc., 2000. pp. 97–110.

Amorosi, Thomas. "Climate Impact and Human Reponse in Northeast Iceland: Archaeological Investigations at Svalbarđ, 1986–1988." *Norse and Later Settlement and Subsistence in the North Atlantic.* Eds. Christopher D. Morris and D. James Rackham. Glasgow: University of Glasgow, 1992. pp. 103–138.

Bell, Trevor, Joyce B. Macpherson, and M.A.P. Renouf. "'Wish you were here...': A Thumbnail Portrait of the Great Northern Peninsula AD 1000." *Vínland Revisited: The Norse World at the Turn of the First Millennium, Selected papers from the Viking Millennium International Symposium, Sept. 15-24, Newfoundland and Labrador.* Ed. Shannon Lewis-Simpson. St. John's: Historic Sites Association of Newfoundland and Labrador, Inc., 2000. pp. 203–218.

Berglund, Joel. 2000. "The Farm Beneath the Sand." *Vikings: The North Atlantic Saga.* Eds. William Fitzhugh and Elisabeth I. Ward. Smithsonian Books, Washington D.C., 2000. pp. 295–303.

Buckland, Paul C. "The North Atlantic Environment." *Vikings: The North Atlantic Saga.* Eds. William Fitzhugh and Elisabeth I. Ward. Smithsonian Books, Washington D.C., 2000. pp. 146–153.

--. "The North Atlantic Farm: An Environmental View." *The Viking World.* Eds. Stefan Brink and Neil Price. New York: Routledge, 2008. pp. 598–603.

Buckland, Paul C., Kevin L. Edwards, Eva Panagiotakopulu and J. Edward Schofield. "Paleoecological and historical evidence for manuring and irrigation at *Garđar* (Igaliku), Norse Eastern Settlement, Greenland." *The Holocene.* 19 (2009) 1. pp. 105–116.

Christensen, Arne Emil, Jr. "Test Excavations of the Boat-Sheds." *The Norse Discovery of America: Excavations of a Norse Settlement at L'Anse aux Meadows, Newfoundland 1961–1968.* Ed. Anne Stine Ingstad. Trans. Elizabeth Seeberg. Oslo: Universitetsforlaget. New York: Oxford University Press, 1985. Vol. 1 of 2. pp. 86–97.

--. "Ships and Navigation." *Vikings: The North Atlantic Saga.* Eds. William Fitzhugh and Elisabeth I. Ward. Smithsonian Books, Washington D.C., 2000. pp. 86–97.

Edwards, Kevin J., J. Edward Schofield, & Dmitri Marqouy. "High resolution paleoenvironmental and chronological investigations of Norse *landnám* at Tasiusaq, Eastern Settlement, Greenland." *Quaternary Research.* 69 (2008). pp. 1–15.

"Eirik the Red's Saga." Trans. Keneva Kunz. *The Vinland Sagas: The Icelandic Sagas about the First Documented Voyages across the North Atlantic.* New York: Penguin Books, 2008. pp. 25–50.

Eldjárn, Kristján. "Investigations." *The Norse Discovery of America: Excavations of a Norse Settlement at L'Anse aux Meadows, Newfoundland 1961–1968.* Ed. Anne Stine Ingstad. Trans. Elizabeth Seeberg. Oslo: Universitetsforlaget. New York: Oxford University Press, 1985. Vol. 1 of 2. pp. 97–107.

Gad, Finn. *The History of Greenland I: Earliest Times to 1700.* Trans. Ernst Dupont. London: C. Hurst & Company, 1970.

Hamilton, J. R. C. *Excavations at Jarlshof, Shetland.* Ministry of Works Archaeological Reports No. 1. Edinburgh, Her Majesty's Stationary Office, 1956.

Henningsmoen, Kari E. "Pollen-analytical Investigation in the L'Anse aux Meadows Area, Newfoundland." *The Norse Discovery of America: Excavations of a Norse Settlement at L'Anse aux Meadows, Newfoundland 1961–1968* Ed. Anne Stine Ingstad. Trans. Elizabeth Seeberg. Oslo: Universitetsforlaget. New York: Oxford University Press, 1985. Vol. 1 of 2. pp. 309–362.

Ingstad, Anne Stine, ed. [A. Ingstad 1985]. *The Norse Discovery of America: Excavations of a Norse Settlement at L'Anse aux Meadows, Newfoundland 1961–1968.* Trans. Elizabeth Seeberg. Oslo: Universitetsforlaget. New York: Oxford University Press, 1985. Vol. 1 of 2. pp. 25–29.

--. [1985a]. "Introduction." *The Norse Discovery of America: Excavations of a Norse Settlement at L'Anse aux Meadows, Newfoundland 1961-1968*. Ed. Anne Stine Ingstad. Trans. Elizabeth Seeberg. Oslo: Universitetsforlaget. New York: Oxford University Press, 1985. Vol. 1 of 2. pp. 25-29.

--. [1985b]. "Investigations." *The Norse Discovery of America: Excavations of a Norse Settlement at L'Anse aux Meadows, Newfoundland 1961–1968*. Ed. Anne Stine Ingstad. Trans. Elizabeth Seeberg. Oslo: Universitetsforlaget. New York: Oxford University Press, 1985. Vol. 1 of 2. pp. 29–56, 73–95.

--. [1985c]. "Cultural Affinities." *The Norse Discovery of America: Excavations of a Norse Settlement at L'Anse aux Meadows, Newfoundland 1961–1968*. Ed. Anne Stine Ingstad. Trans. Elizabeth Seeberg. Oslo: Universitetsforlaget. New York: Oxford University Press, 1985. Vol. 1 of 2. pp. 151–253.

--. [1985d]. "Conclusion." *The Norse Discovery of America: Excavations of a Norse Settlement at L'Anse aux Meadows, Newfoundland 1961–1968*. Ed. Anne Stine Ingstad. Trans. Elizabeth Seeberg. Oslo: Universitetsforlaget. New York: Oxford University Press, 1985. Vol. 1 of 2. pp. 255–268.

Ingstad, Helge. "Norse Sites at L'Anse aux Meadows." *The Quest for America*. Ed. Geoffrey Ashe. NewYork: Praeger Publishers, 1971.

--. *The Vikings and America*. New York: Thames and Hudson, Inc., 1986.

Ingstad, Helge and Anne Stine Ingstad. *The Viking Discovery of America: The Excavation of a Norse Settlement in L'Anse aux Meadows, Newfoundland*. St. John's: Breakwater Books Ltd, 2000.

Jóhannesson, Jón. *Íslendinga saga: A History of the Old Icelandic Commonwealth*. Trans. by Haraldur Bessason. University of Manitoba Press, 2006.

Lewis-Simpson, Shannon. "Introduction: Approaches and Arguments." *Vínland Revisited: The Norse World at the Turn of the First Millennium, Selected papers from the Viking Millennium International Symposium, Sept. 15–24, Newfoundland and Labrador*. Ed. Shannon Lewis-Simpson. St. John's: Historic Sites Association of Newfoundland and Labrador, Inc., 2000. pp. 21–26.

Lynnerup, Niels, and Nina Von Wowern. "Bone Mineral Content in Medieval Greenland Norse." *International Journal of Osteoarchaeology*. 7 (1970). pp. 235–240.

Magnusson, Magnus, KBE. "Vínland: the Ultimate Outpost." *Vínland Revisited: The Norse World at the Turn of the First Millennium, Selected papers from the Viking Millennium International Symposium, Sept. 15–24, Newfoundland and Labrador*. Ed. Shannon Lewis-Simpson. St. John's: Historic Sites Association of Newfoundland and Labrador, Inc., 2000. pp. 83–96.

Mc Govern, Thomas H., Sophia Perdikaris, and Clayton Tinsley. "The Economy of *Landnám*: The Evidence of Zooarchaeology." *Approaches to Vínland: a conference on the written and archaeological sources for the Norse settlements in the North-Atlantic region and exploration of America*. Reykjavík: Sigurður Nordal Institute, 2000. pp. 154–65.

Nörlund, Poul, and Märten Stenberger. *Brattahlid*. Researches into Norse Culture in Greenland, Bd. 88, Nr. 1. Copenhagen: C.A. Reitzels Forlag, 1934.

Ólafsson, Haradlur. "Introduction: Sagas of Western Expansion." *Vikings: The North Atlantic Saga*. Eds. William Fitzhugh and Elisabeth I. Ward. Smithsonian Books, Washington D.C., 2000. pp. 143–145.

Østergård, Else. *Woven into the Earth: Textiles from Norse Greenland*. Aarhus University Press: Aarhus, Denmark, 2004.

Perdikaris, Sophia, and Thomas H. McGovern. "Cod Fish, Walrus, and Chieftains: Economic intensification in the Norse North Atlantic." *Seeking a Richer Harvest: The Archaeology of Subsistence Intensification, Innovation, and Change*. Eds. Tina L. Thurston and Christopher T. Fisher. New York: Springer, 2007. pp. 193–216.

Petré, Rolf. "Investigations 18th-27th July 1962." *The Norse Discovery of America: Excavations of a Norse Settlement at L'Anse aux Meadows, Newfoundland 1961–1968*. Ed. Anne Stine Ingstad. Trans. Elizabeth Seeberg. Oslo: Universitetsforlaget. New York: Oxford University Press, 1985. Vol. 1 of 2. pp. 59–71.

Pleiner, Radomír. *Iron in Archaeology: The European Blooming Shelters*. Praha: Archaeologický ústav AVČR, 2000.

Rothery, Agnes. *Iceland: New World Outpost*. New York: The Viking Press, 1948.

"The Saga of the Greenlanders." Trans. Keneva Kunz. *The Vinland Sagas: The Icelandic Sagas about the First Documented Voyages across the*

North Atlantic. New York: Penguin Books, 2008. pp. 3–21.

Sawyer, Birgit. "Scandinavia in the Viking Age." *Vínland Revisited: The Norse World at the Turn of the First Millennium, Selected papers from the Viking Millennium International Symposium, Sept. 15–24, Newfoundland and Labrador.* Ed. Shannon Lewis-Simpson. St. John's: Historic Sites Association of Newfoundland and Labrador, Inc., 2000. pp. 51–64

--. "Women in Viking-Age Scandinavia, or, who were the 'shieldmaidens'?" *Vínland Revisited: The Norse World at the Turn of the First Millennium, Selected papers from the Viking Millennium International Symposium, Sept. 15–24, Newfoundland and Labrador.* Ed. Shannon Lewis-Simpson. St. John's: Historic Sites Association of Newfoundland and Labrador, Inc., 2000. pp. 295–304.

Schofield, J. Edward, Kevin J. Edwards, and Charlie Christensen. "Environmental impacts around the time of Norse *landnám* in the Qorlortoq valley, Eastern Settlement, Greenland. *Journal of Archaeological Science*. 35 (2008) pp. 1643–1657.

Schonback, Bengt, Birgitta Wallace and Charles Lindsay. "The Progress Report on Archaeological Fieldwork at L'Anse aux Meadows, June to October, 1975. *Research Bulletin, National Historic Parks and Sites Branch*. Parks Canada, Department of Indian and Northern Affairs. No. 33. July 1976.

Shetelig, Haakon, and Hjalmar Falk. 1978. *Scandinavian Archaeology*. New York: Hacker Art Books, Inc.

Smith, Kevin. "*Landnám*: the settlement of Iceland in archaeological and historical perspective." *World Archaeology*. 26 (Feb. 1995, *Colonization of Islands*) 3. pp. 319–347.

--. "Ore, Fire, Hammer, Sickle: Iron Production in Viking Age and Early Medieval Iceland." *De re metallica: the uses of metal in the Middle Ages*. Eds. Robert Bork et al. Burlinton, VT: Ashgate, 2005.

Vésteinsson, Orri. "The Archaeology of *Landnám*." *Vikings: The North Atlantic Saga*. Eds. William Fitzhugh and Elisabeth I. Ward. Smithsonian Books, Washington D.C., 2000. pp. 164–174.

Vésteinsson, Orri, Thomas H. McGovern & Christian Keller. "Enduring Impacts: Social and Environmental Aspects of Viking Age Settlement in Iceland and Greenland." *Archaeologia Islandica*. 2 (2002). pp. 98–136.

Wallace, Birgitta. "The Norse in Newfoundland." *Conservation Canada*. Summer 1977. pp. 3–7.

--. "The 1976 Excavations at L'Anse aux Meadows, Newfoundland." *Research Bulletin, National Historic Parks and Sites Branch*. Parks Canada, Department of Indian and Northern Affairs. No. 67. November 1977.

--."L'Anse aux Meadows: Gateway to Vinland." *The Norse of the North Atlantic. Acta Archaeologica*. 61 (1990). Copenhagen, 1991. pp. 166–197.

--. [2000a]. "The later excavations at L'Anse aux Meadows." *Vínland Revisited: The Norse World at the Turn of the First Millennium, Selected papers from the Viking Millennium International Symposium, Sept. 15-24, Newfoundland and Labrador*. Ed. Shannon Lewis-Simpson. St. John's: Historic Sites Association of Newfoundland and Labrador, Inc., 2000. pp. 165–180.

--. [2000b]. "Vínland and the death of Þorvaldr." *Vínland Revisited: The Norse World at the Turn of the First Millennium, Selected papers from the Viking Millennium International Symposium, Sept. 15-24, Newfoundland and Labrador*. Ed. Shannon Lewis-Simpson. St. John's: Historic Sites Association of Newfoundland and Labrador, Inc., 2000. pp. 377–390.

--. [2000c]. "The Viking Settlement at L'Anse aux Meadows." *Vikings: The North Atlantic Saga*. Eds. William Fitzhugh and Elisabeth I. Ward. Smithsonian Books, Washington D.C, 2000. pp. 208–216.

--. *Westward Vikings: The Saga of L'Anse aux Meadows*. St. John's: Historic Sites Association of Newfoundland and Labrador, 2006.

Zutter, Cynthia. "Icelandic Plant and Land-use Patterns: Archaeobotanical Analysis of the Svalbarð Midden (6706-60), Northeastern Iceland." *Norse and Later Settlement and Subsistence in the North Atlantic*. Eds. Christopher D. Morris and D. James Rackham. Glasgow: University of Glasgow, 1992. pp. 139–148.

www.ingramcontent.com/pod-product-compliance
Lightning Source LLC
Chambersburg PA
CBHW061549010526
44115CB00023B/2996